T0286361

human
design

human design

The revolutionary system that shows you who you came here to be

jenna zoë

HAY HOUSE
Carlsbad, California • New York City
London • Sydney • New Delhi

Published in the United Kingdom by:
Hay House UK Ltd, The Sixth Floor, Watson House, 54 Baker Street,
London W1U 7BU; Tel: +44 (0)20 3927 7290; www.hayhouse.co.uk

Published in the United States of America by:
Hay House Inc., PO Box 5100, Carlsbad, CA 92018-5100
Tel: (1) 760 431 7695 or (800) 654 5126; www.hayhouse.com

Published in Australia by:
Hay House Australia Pty Ltd, 18/36 Ralph St, Alexandria NSW 2015
Tel: (61) 2 9669 4299; www.hayhouse.com.au

Published in India by:
Hay House Publishers India, Muskaan Complex, Plot No.3, B-2, Vasant Kunj,
New Delhi 110 070; Tel: (91) 11 4176 1620; www.hayhouse.co.in

A catalogue record for this book is available from the British Library.

Tradepaper ISBN: 978-1-4019-7119-9
E-book ISBN: 978-1-78817-885-3
Audiobook ISBN: 978-1-78817-886-0

12 11 10 9 8 7 6 5 4 3

Printed in the United States of America

This product uses papers sourced from responsibly managed forests.
For more information, see www.hayhouse.com.

Daring to be the real you is the adventure of a lifetime.

Contents

A Note for the Reader ix

Introduction xi

Chapter 1: Your Human Design Chart 1

Chapter 2: Your Energy Type 7

Chapter 3: Your Strategy 41

Chapter 4: Your Signature and Not-Self 53

Chapter 5: Your Authority 65

Chapter 6: Your Profile 85

Chapter 7: Your Gifts 133

Conclusion: Living Your Design 281

Acknowledgments 285

About the Author 287

A Note for the Reader

The traditional rules of grammar and punctuation have not been applied to this text to preserve the unique and inspirational voice of the author. In her own words:

> *'I chose to write these words as I would say them to you if we were together, having a conversation. So it's more informal and colloquial than the traditional tone books are written in, but with the intention that it really lands in your Spirit.'*
>
> JENNA ZOË

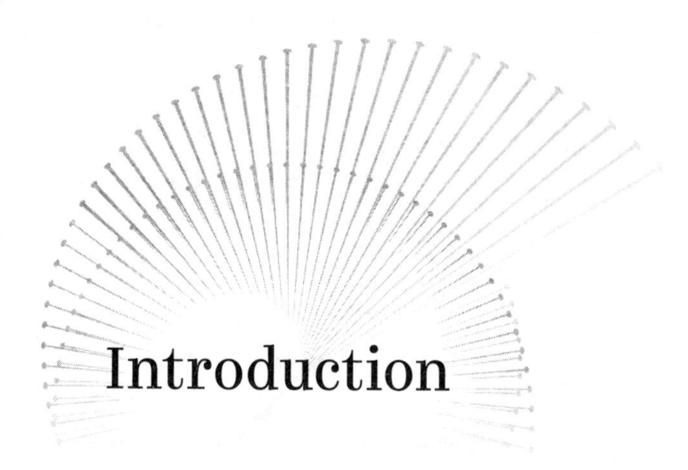

Introduction

The world is changing – fast. And if you've come to this book, you've probably looked around at the current ways of thinking, doing, and operating and thought – maybe it's not set up in a way that enables us to thrive.

Whether you look as close as your best friend or at the wider global situation, we could all be more fulfilled, to say the least.

And the way we're going to get there is not with a cookie-cutter, 'six steps to fulfillment' plan.

Human Design is a system that says that first you learn how a person is specifically built, then design their optimal way of being from there. We all know we're totally different, so it makes sense that our blueprint to success, ease, and purpose are different too.

We need to start recognizing our individuality and working *with* it rather than trying to squeeze ourselves into a homogenous strategy – and then thinking there's something wrong with *us* when it doesn't work!

Before your Soul comes here, it decides exactly the path it wants to accomplish in this life. And in order to help it do and have and become all the things it wants to in this incarnation, it chooses the exact ways of being that would help it do all that.

Your ways of being are not random; they are Divine.

Using your birth time, date, and place, we can use Human Design to pinpoint your exact gifts, traits, and ideal ways of being and living.

Think about the moment you're born – every place and time has an energy. Your Soul chooses the exact energy it needs as the perfect launchpad for your life – so your birth information tells us about who you inherently are.

The day you are born, you're already living how your Highest Self would live; the goal is to identify it and be true to *that* rather than how you've been told you need to be. Your conditioning is all the stuff you became that was never really You to begin with, and this process is about deconditioning – not becoming anything, but about unbecoming everything you were told to be in the first place.

It can be hard to know Who We Really Are when we've spent so much of our lives being conditioned to be otherwise; that's why it really helps to have a science outside ourselves to help us measure it.

And the Universe has designed each of us to be exactly how we need to be – not just to fulfill our own dreams, but also so that our society, together, can function most beautifully, harmoniously, and have everything it needs provided by someone. The more everyone fully lives their special skills and Essence, the higher heights we can reach as a collective. This is what they mean when they say you serve a purpose here – you are perfectly designed to fill your specific role.

And the jig is – you don't know your role before you start – you embrace your skills, and your role unfolds right in front of your eyes. Sure, Mozart knew at age 3 he was a composer, but that's because he had to for his path. But Life is *designed* to make more and more sense as it goes along, even if you think you know early on how it's all going to unfold.

One thing I know for sure is when you let your natural inclinations dictate where you go and how you go, they will take you to a stratospheric manifestation of your potential. Because you can only become your Highest Self, by first actually *being* yourself. So it's time to stop making yourself be anything you've been told you have to be to live a dream life, and just be who you came here to be.

Daring to be the real you is the adventure of a lifetime.

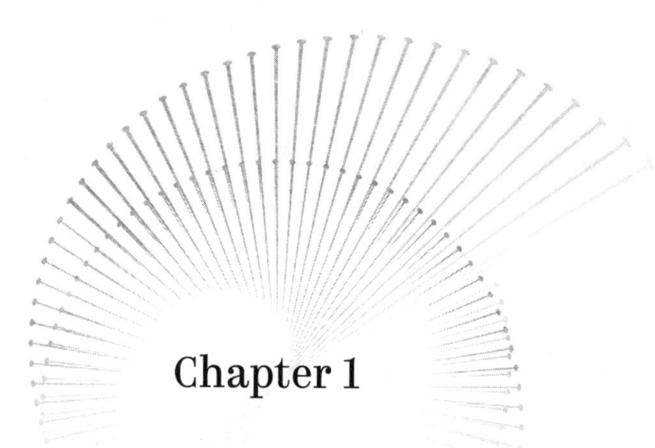

Chapter 1

Your Human Design Chart

When you come into this world, you are seeded with the energy that was in the Universe at that time. If we can measure that energy, we can measure exactly the energy your Soul chose to embody.

In 1987 a man named Ra Uru Hu created a system that would do just that. Combining aspects of astrology, the I Ching, the chakra system, and the Kabbalistic Tree of Life, he created a way of measuring exactly who you are with Human Design.

Every Human Design journey starts by looking up your Human Design chart.

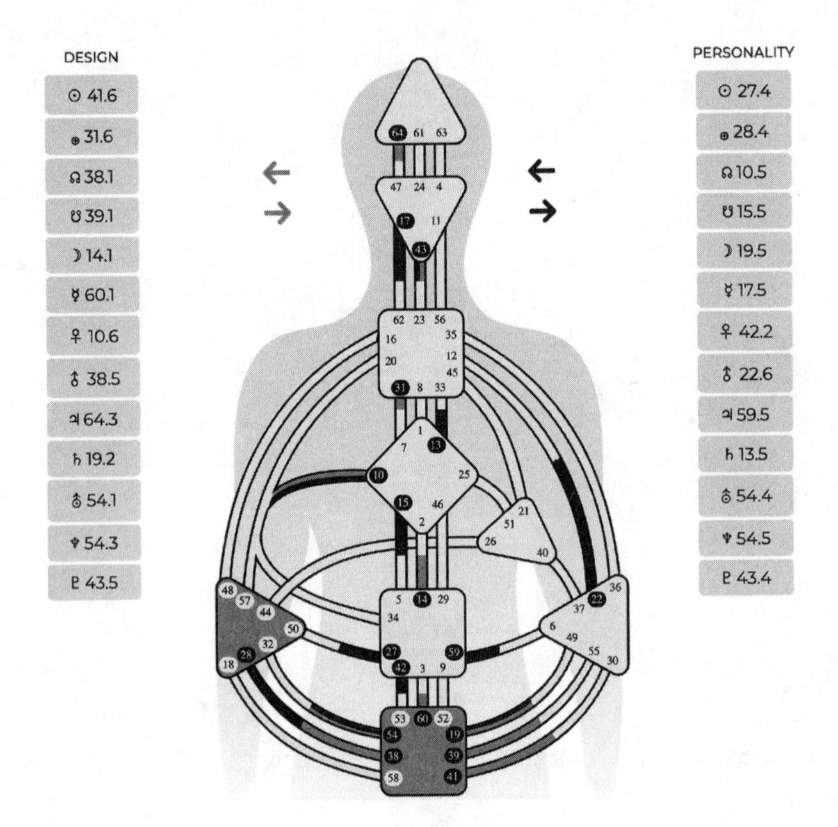

An example Human Design chart

Looking Up Your Chart

In order to look up your design, visit www.myhumandesign.com or scan this code, and enter your birth information.

You will need your birth day, place, year, and time. The exact time really matters because even being born five minutes later can make differences – sometimes big, sometimes small.

If you don't know your exact birth time:

- It should be on your birth certificate if you're born in the United States and certain other countries too.
- You can also call the hospital where you were born and ask them to share or send your birth records to you.
- If you think you were born between, say, 8 a.m. and 9 a.m., you can enter various times within that hour and see what changes and how much – then focus on those things that remain consistent within that hour. Sometimes it changes very little, sometimes it can change your Energy Type completely.
- If you're really stuck, you can also do something called astrological rectification, which some very talented astrologers offer – they work backward based on your current life experience and nail down the exact birth time from there. It's wild, but amazing!

We also have an app, My Human Design, which you can find here:

You can run unlimited charts and keep them on your phone. It includes a full description of each person, both audio and written.

Reading the Map of Your Energy

A chart is simply a map of your energy. Everyone has a physical body and also an energy body. It's like an energetic billboard that introduces you everywhere you go. It contains all the information about your Essence and what you're good at, and people feel that when they're around you, whether they know it or not.

When you walk into a room, if what you're advertising yourself as is the same as what your energy is advertising you as, these are people who come across as strong magnetic people – because their soul and their surface are on the same page.

Living Your Design

Living your Design means you make choices that are Aligned with how your system is designed to function. The following are the main layers, which we will cover in this book:

- Your Energy Type – how your energy flows
- Your Strategy – how you make things happen most easily and effortlessly
- Your Signature and Not-Self – the ways the Universe shows you when you're in and out of Alignment a.k.a. 'on the right track'
- Your Authority – how to always know the right decision for you

- Your Profile – your persona/personality
- Your Gifts – the things you are naturally good at

When you put all these things together, they give you a picture of how to live as your Real Self, rather than as the constructed self, the one that was handed to you by outside expectations.

The Ethos of Human Design

Let's say your Soul is here to bring people together; the more you're consciously aware of that, own it, and then do it, the more Easy Success it creates for you, because you're communicating to the world exactly what you are – most of the time without needing to speak it. So people know what to come to you for, and everything that the Universe sends you is fielded correctly.

If there was nothing else you did, and you just focused on following your Strategy and Authority, you'll inevitably start living all the other parts of your Design, even if you don't know them, because you're steering your vehicle right at every junction. So your path unfolds the way it's meant to, meaning everything within you also falls into place.

Ignoring the Mind's Opinions

Everyone's mind has come here to accomplish uncommon levels of genius, wisdom, and expertise – and then share them with the world. This will be your unique contribution that only your Essence can ever produce. In Human Design our minds were designed for us to use on the outside world, but we can't use them on that because we are using them up on the everyday aspects of our personal lives.

We've been conditioned to turn our minds inward – and this is the source of so much of our suffering. The mind will spin out so much excess worry, anxiety, and fear when it's tasked on our own selves. Turn it outward, watch it soar – you will be surprised at how much more bright and sharp your mind and your perceptions of life become.

Since your mind is polluted with ideas about what is you, what is right for you, what will work out well and what won't – you can't rely on it to steer you toward your highest most powerful expression because it was never designed for that in the first place.

As for your own life path, let something else take care of it – your Strategy and Authority. They can steer you so much better than your mind ever will, because that's their playing field.

With everything you're about to read, play it out in your life – don't ask your mind to figure out if this is true or not, but play it out and watch the results. Every single human trait is actually neutral – each has a positive expression and a negative expression of itself. It's our consciousness we do things with that determines which expression will come out. So try not to judge the qualities we'll be discussing here as 'good' or 'bad' ones to have, because doing so keeps us locked into who we've told ourselves we need to be rather than taking the leap into who we could be.

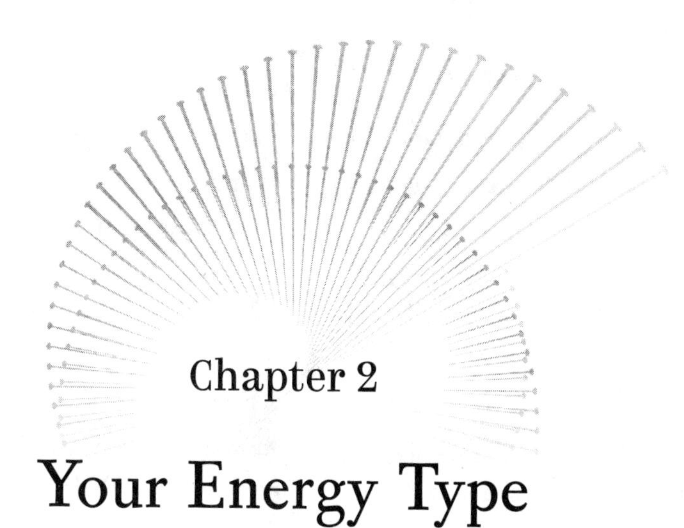

Chapter 2

Your Energy Type

The starting point in Human Design is your Energy Type – it's like asking someone their sun sign in astrology.

Your Energy Type describes the unique way you're meant to operate in this world: your energy levels, energy patterns, and your ways of doing, resting, and, most importantly – where and how your energy reaps the most rewards and returns. Everyone has different ways they are meant to do things, and your Energy Type tells you your best one.

Too often, we try to 'do things' the way we think we should do them, the way we've been told works best for everyone. But you always know you're going against your Energy Type when you're putting so much energy and effort in, but not getting anywhere. Or you're exhausted and depleted and unhappy.

But when you honor your natural ways instead of trying to do things how you think you should, everything in your life comes together more easily, effortlessly, and successfully.

Say for example you get big bursts of energy but then need to completely stop to majorly recoup, then working a consistent nine-to-five where you do the same amount of energy every day isn't going to work for you.

Maybe the world tells you that's the only way to be successful, but that's ironically what's holding you back, because it's not the way the Universe designed you to get to your best life.

Right now, we're only just starting to see how alternative work and life patterns are helping people thrive and live their dreams all over the world.

It starts with getting to know how you function and trusting that over any of the 'shoulds' and prefabricated molds the world is asking you to fit into.

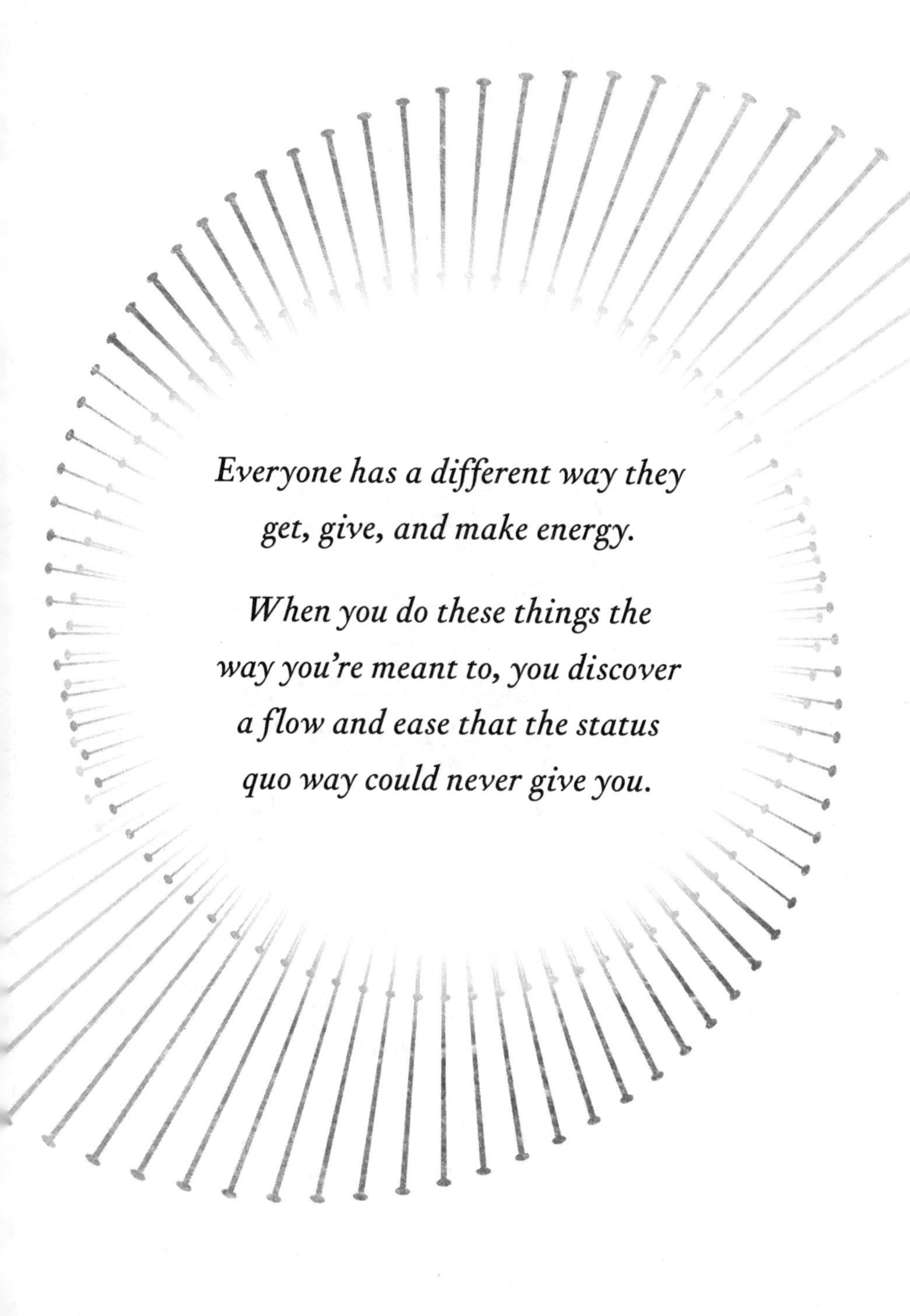

Everyone has a different way they get, give, and make energy.

When you do these things the way you're meant to, you discover a flow and ease that the status quo way could never give you.

Manifestor

A Manifestor has an undefined Sacral center,
and at least one of the Emotional, Ego, or Root
centers defined and connected to the Throat.

The Essence of a Manifestor

Manifestors are wild, strong, playful creatures

As a Manifestor, you were born with a very strong sense of who you wanted to be; you were born already knowing how to raise yourself.

But it's likely that the adults in your life were told to discipline and regulate your natural urges because that's what they were told is the right thing to do with kids. But on you, discipline actually constricts your energy by telling you it's not good to be a wild, spontaneous, strong creature – when that's exactly what you came here to be.

Not only are you *meant* to be like that – but that's actually when people will love you the most, even if they don't know that consciously. That's also when you'll be most successful, impactful, and feel most at peace in yourself.

Even though you may have been praised for being obedient and abandoning your own wants, giving yourself the license to do whatever the eff you want is your role in this lifetime.

The Role of a Manifestor

To create movement

As a Manifestor, you're an initiator – you get the ball rolling, start something, create movement (often without even trying) that others can then join in on or follow you on. You don't have to 'figure out' how to create movements – you just have to follow your urges, because those are the very things that will create the right impetus in others. When you're being fully you, your actions will always create a spark in others that they can then react to. What you do and create will stir something in others, and the right ones will flock to get on your train. This is you – you are the cause, and everyone else is the effect.

Doing what you want

The thing about creating new movements is that others are never gonna understand them before you've actually gone ahead and done it. So it starts with you giving yourself the license to go off and be and do what your heart is leading you to do, trusting that that's always the way you're going to create everything you want.

When you just give yourself permission to do what you want to do, this gets the right people on board without you even trying. Your Essence has a self-selection mechanism that sifts people into three different buckets for the best outcome to take place. In the first, people will be drawn right to you because they need and want this kind of essence in their lives – these are people who will want to follow and partake in whatever it is you create. For others, it will ruffle their feathers, because you're shaking them awake. When this is a natural by-product of you just doing your thing, this is actually a very healthy thing for those people to feel for their own evolution. And others, who simply aren't meant to come along for the ride of whatever your urges are leading you to do, will not react at all.

Your biggest desire is to be able to do exactly what you want. Manifestors are unintentional leaders, because, ironically, when they do whatever they want and let themselves be seen doing it, it catches the attention of the very people who are meant to partake in it. So when you go off and do your own thing, breaking off from the pack, you end up creating a much more beneficial, Aligned version of a pack. A higher, better option for others to come join you on. You long to feel supported more than anything, and it's actually when you stop doing the things you think you have to do and say to give you support and instead do what your urges are calling you to do, you receive the truest, most devoted kind of support, adoration, and acceptance. Because your urges are leading you to do something that would be so life enhancing for other people too. Stepping into your bigness is your job, because other people need it more than you, or they, realize yet.

Think of yourself as a train driver – you tell people where the train is going and what time it's leaving, and then whoever wants to be part of it gets on board. You don't get off the train and ask everyone on the platform where they'd like to go – because you'd go nowhere trying to please everybody!

Manifestor Energy Patterns

Manifestor energy is not constant, it comes in surges

Since you're an initiator, you are not built to have a consistent level of energy all day long; instead your energy works in bursts. You're at 200 percent when you're doing and creating, and then you need to go

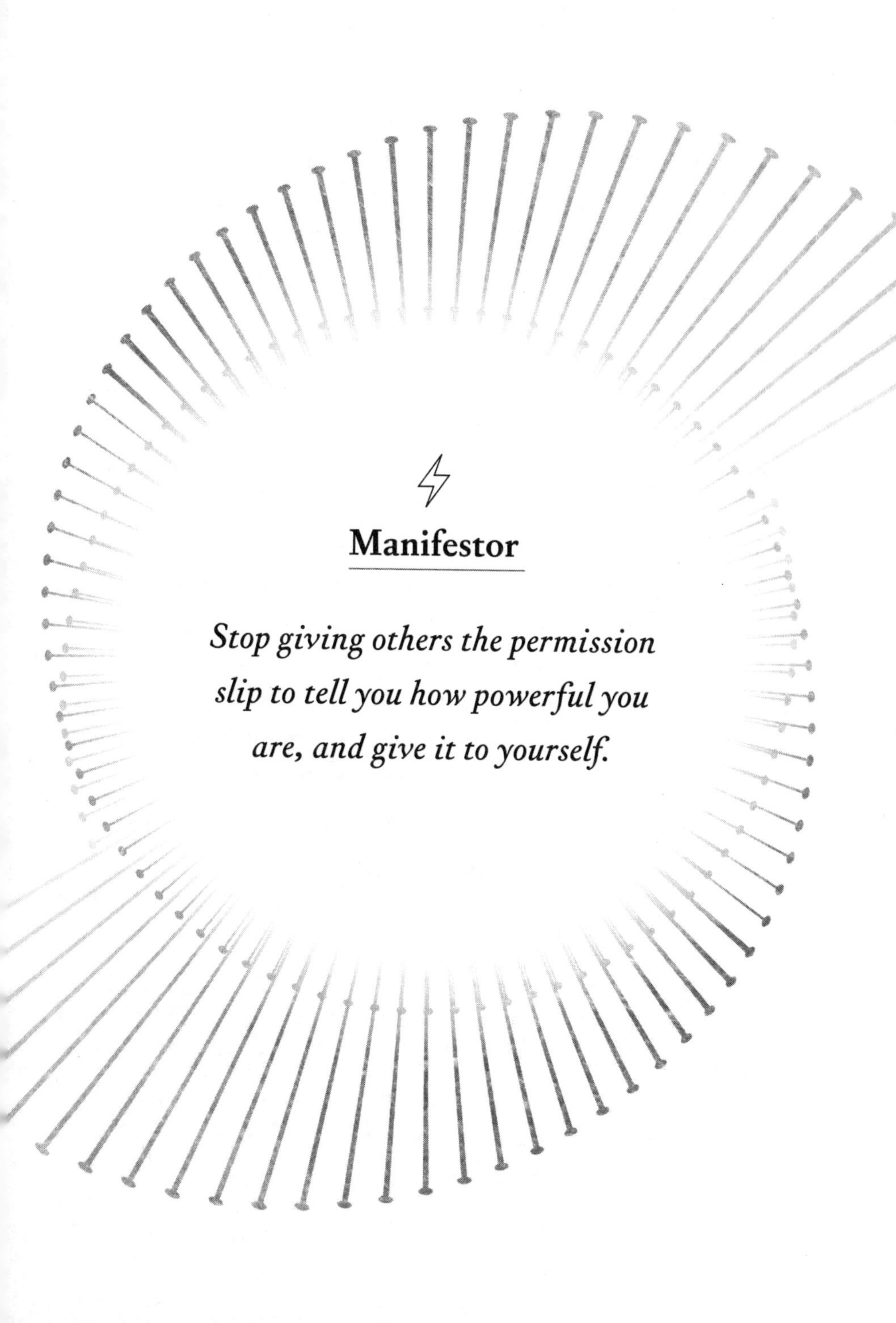

Manifestor

Stop giving others the permission slip to tell you how powerful you are, and give it to yourself.

to 50 percent or 20 percent so you can rest and prepare for the next project. The Universe directs you by sending you urges – spontaneous fancies that come to you, telling you what to do next in life. When you are overcome by an urge, the Universe gives it to you with a surge of energy to carry it out. Once you've carried out that urge, you then need to rest and reset until you feel an urge to do the next thing. You're not built to have the consistent energy for a nine-to-five day, you're built for peaks and valleys. In the peaks, you have an abundance of energy and power, and then when you've finished carrying out your urge, you need to come back to yourself. When you let yourself flow with this is actually when everything you do will have the most power. Like fire, if you burn slowly all day it won't make much of an impact. But if you set something alight and have it become engulfed in a fireball even for a short while, other people will notice, and the fire will catch on.

Once you've acted on an urge, it causes a ripple effect in the world that you can't control – and you're not here to micromanage how others react to what you do. Once you've done the thing that sets your Soul alight, let it go and let the sparks fly wherever they fly.

How to Get Aligned as a Manifestor

Embrace your bigness

Bigness is scary because it's so misunderstood: it's not loud, aggressive, or in your face. It's just unafraid to stand in its own Essence and radiate that out in the world instead of adapting and changing for anyone. Trust that your Essence is perfect, because it's the Essence the Universe designed for you specifically, so it's something to honor rather than be ashamed of or apologetic for.

If it helps, don't think of your Essence as 'you'; it's on loan to you for this lifetime so that you can enjoy it and share it with others. The secret to living a good life is trusting that exactly what you're inclined to do and be will change other people's lives for the better when you simply become fully okay with all the different aspects of it.

The second you stand fully unapologetic in your Essence, people will take notice. And people noticing you is the very thing that activates your Purpose as a Manifestor.

You don't have to try to be big...

Manifestors sense deep down they're here to impact other people, but the world tells them they need to figure out 'how' to do this. In reality it happens as a natural side effect when you're following your urges. When you do whatever the hell you want, when you're doing what makes you feel alive, that's when everybody wins. The reason it can be difficult to embrace this is because society has taught us that, in order to help others, we have to sacrifice our own wants. In reality, it's actually by being the truest expression of ourselves that we will be the most beneficial to others. The Universe is built on a win-win principle like that.

Your energy is intense and big, in a good way. Think of when something comes over you so strongly that it moves you, and it changes the direction of your life; this is you at your highest expression. You mustn't take it personally when your loved ones can't keep up with your level of intensity, because they weren't built for that same role as you. If what you did *wasn't* intense and impactful, it wouldn't wake people up enough, and it needs to be able to do that. Intense is good and beautiful for you when you just go off and do what makes you happy – because it's the happiness that becomes intensified. And how magnetic is a person with big energy who is in their joy, at peace with themselves, and Aligned? It's the kind of person that shifts worlds.

... you just have to stop being small

Throughout your life, though, you've probably received a lot of messages that tell you it's better to smallen your nature. So many Manifestors end up becoming overly apologetic, doubtful of who they are, or spend their energy trying to people-please rather than spend it on doing the things their hearts would do if they 100 percent trusted in themselves.

Manifestors also feel criticism and judgment from others deeply, and this causes them to not share what they're up to or to want to distance themselves from people. They fear being seen because they equate that automatically with having to handle scrutiny; but know that doesn't have to be the case. Know that when you are fully okay with being you, you attract a life where you are met with approval, reverence, and support.

Any smallening in your energy blocks the magnificence of who you really are from being felt by others, and by you in yourself. So if you're living your life in a way that's so Aligned, but you still feel like you could be having so much more impact and success, simply focus on getting rid of the fear of being seen and let yourself shine.

Generator

A Generator has a defined Sacral center, but neither the Sacral, Heart, Emotional, nor Root center directly connected to the Throat by a full colored channel.

The Essence of a Generator

A Generator's Purpose is to create good energy in the world

As the name suggests, you are here to *generate* energy: whenever you do something that makes you happy, excited, and Lit up, you create so much good energy that it radiates out of you – and everyone around you benefits or feels it. Being Lit up is your highest calling because when you're happy and excited, that spillover of good energy inspires, fuels, and lifts everyone else up around you – without you even trying.

Generators are here to become masters of their craft or passion. When they devote themselves to doing something they love, humble step after humble step, it compounds into an inconceivably good result, and suddenly, they've wound up at their dreams and reaching the top of their game without really knowing how.

Generators have open, inviting auras which draw other people in toward them. When you're excited about something, you become full of life, and this energy can't help but spill out of you into everything and everyone you come across. This is the magic of a Generator – when a Generator is Lit up, they have such juicy sparkly energy that makes everyone want to be around them even if they can't explain why.

Because of this, when a Generator does what they love, everyone wins.

The Role of a Generator

If you want to live your Purpose, do what Lights you up

If you want to help others, know that the Universe has given you specific passions that you're meant to follow in order to live as your highest version. The things that light you up aren't random – they are specifically exciting *to you* because *you* are the one who's meant to be doing them. Life, for you, really is as simple as giving yourself the permission to do what you love and knowing that that's the best way you'll serve others, even if your logical mind can't see 'how' before you start.

Your lit-up-ness makes other people more energized, excited, productive, and gives them momentum in their own life. No matter what job title you may have on the outside, the real value you're providing is that you're infusing the world with Life Force.

How do you know if something Lights you up?

Excitement and desire comes from your Gut, which is the most important part of a Generator's chart. It's the body part that rules your energy. When something comes your way that's exciting to you, whether that's a meal, a job or a lover, your energy perks up and expands. You can literally *feel* it, in your Gut, in your body, and people around you pick up on that, whether they know it consciously or not. It makes them want to be around you, work with you, buy whatever you're selling, or just hug you. This in turn kicks off a chain of opportunities

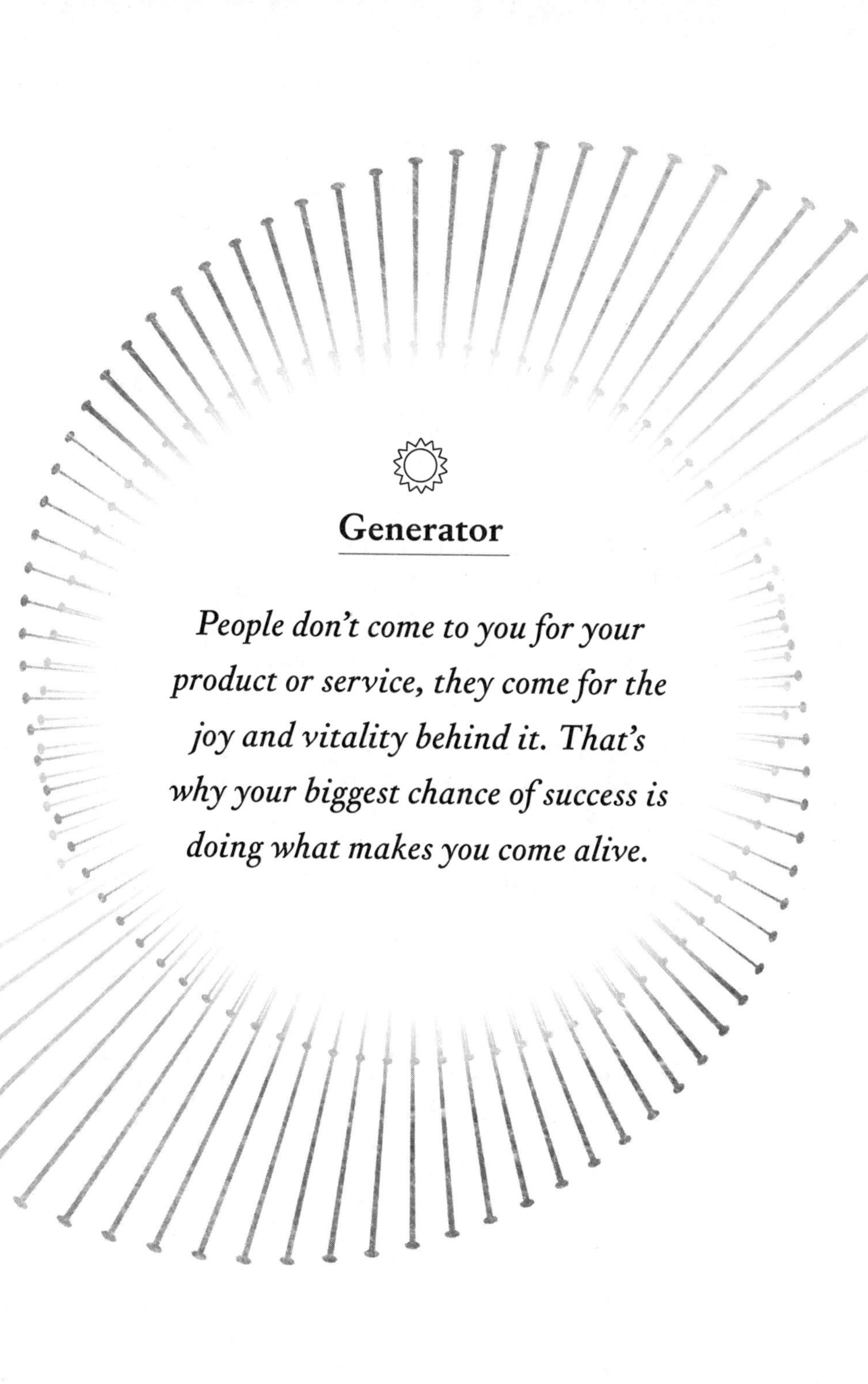

Generator

People don't come to you for your product or service, they come for the joy and vitality behind it. That's why your biggest chance of success is doing what makes you come alive.

and synchronicities between you and the world. So, you don't actually have to figure out what to do in advance. You just have to activate the process by saying yes to what excites you.

Life is constantly sending you things you might like and want; your job is to notice that involuntary excitement response within you and to then reach out and take it. Whether that's to do it, create it, eat it, use it, play with it, buy it, whatever it is. Excitement is always about the action not about the end result. Make sure you do something because it genuinely excites you rather than doing it because you think it's the only way to get an end result that you desire. If you suppress your own happiness because you think you have to in order to get to a certain goal, it will never end well. Because, the truth is, it's not your job to think about end results – if you pave the way there with what makes you happy and excited, you'll create the best outcome even if you don't know what it is.

Ultimately, the things you love to do are the very things that will lead you to your dream life. And you just need to trust that.

Generator Energy Patterns

Do more things that excite you – and fewer things that don't

When you do something you love, you could go and go for hours and only get *more* energized and full of Life. This is the Universe's way of saying do more of this. You get a certain battery at the beginning of your day, use it up on activities that feed you, and when you've run that battery, your head can easily hit the pillow, ready to do the dance again tomorrow.

When you're doing something that you're *not* so jazzed about, you will feel drained and tired. This is Life's way of trying to prevent you from doing more of it and show you that it's not what you're meant to be spending your time on. The biggest conditioning for Generators is the praise you get from others for doing things you don't wanna do – perhaps because it benefits them in some way. For example, your parents said 'Well done' for going to see your grandma when you didn't really want to as a kid, or your friend relies on your Generator energy to help them move home or make a group of people gel together. However, this only backfires because, when you're not excited, you don't create that juicy sparkly energy which is what they actually really want from you. Sure, you can go through the motions of helping them move, but it won't have elevated the energy of the situation for either of you. And if you're not excited to do it, it suggests that the Universe has a better option for the other person too.

How to Get Aligned as a Generator

Saying no

When you trust that your excitement is Divine guidance, it's actually the best thing you can do for everyone involved. When you say no to something because it doesn't light you up, maybe the other person is meant to find someone better suited to help them with it, figure it out themselves and realize they're more capable than they thought, come up with a more creative solution, or be forced to do things in a new way that actually benefits them more. You never know just how you're helping the situation by saying No, but your excitement (or lack thereof) will always lead you to the best outcome.

Saying no clears things off your plate that *don't* Light you up, which creates space in your life for the Universe to start sending you more possibilities of what *does*.

The Universe loves an empty space, because you're sending the signal that you want better, and it will rush to come and help you fill it.

If you're saying yes to everything, there is no space for the things you truly desire to come into your life.

Whenever you're in a place where you want to make changes, you don't have to 'figure out' what new things to do so much as stop keeping yourself busy with all things that don't make you happy. When you create space, you can hear your Soul's true joys.

The fear of doing nothing

The reason why Generators are afraid to start saying no is because of that praise for all the doing they got over the course of their lives – and they're afraid that if they're less busy rushing around even for a hot second, then good things won't come to them. Life wants to see if you're brave enough to go against those false beliefs and be open to working with your joy and not against it.

After removing the No's, you might be less occupied – but it will only be temporary. Use that open space to look around; Life is happening all around you, and it's full of things that might please and delight you. You couldn't see those when you were busying yourself with things you thought you 'had' to do; but now you've opened yourself up to see things that the Universe has been trying to get you to see all along.

Manifesting Generator

Manifesting Generators have a defined Sacral center connected to a defined Throat by a fully colored channel – either directly or through the G center.

The Essence of a Manifesting Generator

Manifesting Generators are multi-passionate people

Manifesting Generators (MGs) are a hybrid of two of the other types, Generators and Manifestors. Like the Generator, doing things that Light them up is what creates energy in the MGs' systems and makes their energy very bright and magnetic to all that's meant for them. But it's blended with the spontaneous, playful nature of the Manifestor, which means they can pivot in new directions out of nowhere. Because of this, they are here to walk through life in a very multi-directional, dynamic, expansive way.

You have various passions and are meant to do many varied things in one lifetime. However, we live in a world that tells you that, in order to be happy or successful, you *have to* choose one lane and stay in it, which is just not true for you. Everything that sparks a passion inside you is trying to get you to follow it, and if you do, it leads you right to everything you desire. Your challenge is to defy what society tells us about how to become happy and successful, and show us a new way of doing it. An MG's gift to the world is to break us out of the boxes we live our lives in and expand our perspective on what's possible.

The Role of a Manifesting Generator

You are here to chart previously unseen life paths

MGs aren't the kind of people who decide they want to be accountants at age 18 and then do it for the rest of their lives. Life, or the Universe, will push an MG to explore many different directions because it wants you to create your own unique blend of passions and turn them into a totally new life path that hasn't yet been seen or done. So, this could mean you switch to a totally new career at least at one point in your life, or you have many different passions and side hustles going at one time, or that you fuse seemingly unrelated things into one career. Just because no one's done it before doesn't mean that you can't create it, and in fact, it's probably why you have to do it.

Manifesting Generators are quick to master new things

When first exploring a passion, MGs get this surge of mastery so that they can quickly pick up a skill or lesson that will serve them farther down the line. For this reason, it's not necessary for them to "finish what they started," or to see something through to the end. Even if you don't know how that lesson or skill will come in handy, trust that it will make sense later. You've been conditioned to put yourself in a box so that the world can understand you and know where you're headed, which makes everyone more comfortable. But your challenge is to defy the pressure to be able to explain where you're going and be okay with the not knowing. When you do this, it blows open the possibilities of what the Universe can then send you.

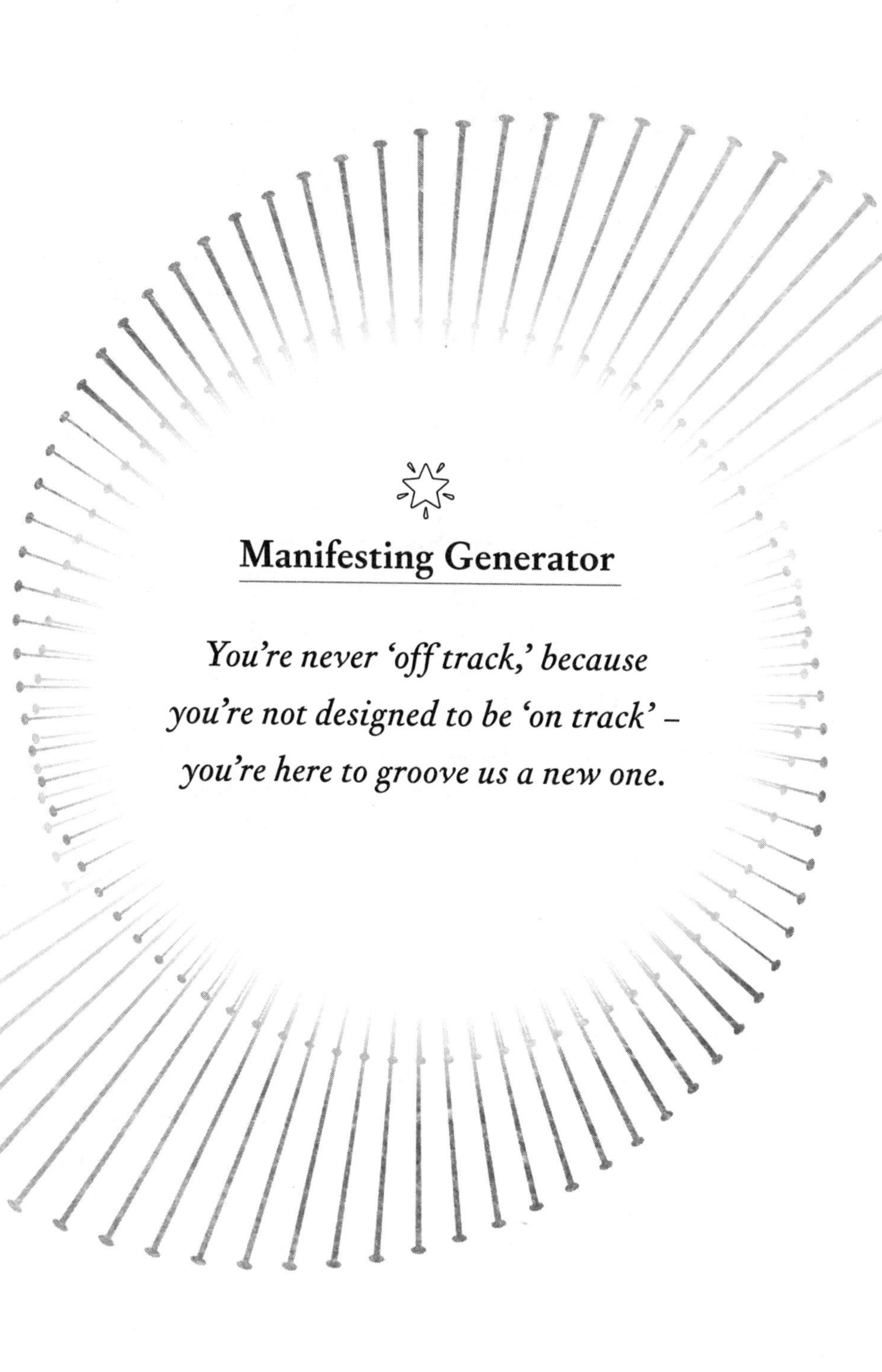

Manifesting Generator

You're never 'off track,' because you're not designed to be 'on track' – you're here to groove us a new one.

Turn the sense of the unknown into a sense of wonder and discovery

Your path is not linear, so it can't be understood before it unfolds. Whenever you feel hesitant or afraid of this unknown, realize that this afraidness only comes because you were conditioned to think that the known is better, is safer, is more of a sure thing. But the *real* sure thing is that you will always get the most fulfilling result when you choose your inside passion over the limited how-tos from the outside world. It's like the Universe implanted your *own* how-to inside you.

At a Soul level, you actually love the unknown because that's what makes life feel like an adventure that surprises and delights you as you live it. Think about it – why would you come here if you already knew exactly how it was gonna pan out? And when you start to love that way of doing Life yourself, you show everyone else that this is *the* way we are all craving to live life. You just have to be stronger than any of us are willing to be and stronger than the voices that try to keep you in the old way. You are here to have more faith in what could be than in what already is.

Manifesting Generator Energy Patterns

As a Manifesting Generator, your energy is spontaneous and in the moment

It can be difficult to decide what will excite you in the future since you are multi-directional. You can only really tell what's exciting to you today, which may well change, so try not to say yes to too many things in your future. This can be difficult as we live in a world that values making plans, commitments, 'sticking with commitments,' and 'knowing what you want.' But that's just not the way you're built to do things.

How to Get Aligned as a Manifesting Generator

Do things you actually want to do

Your passion and desires are signposts, showing you what the Universe wants you to put your attention and energy into. Your wants are not random; and following them is the Highest service you can do in the world.

When you do something that excites you, big or small, you are given more energy so you can keep doing that thing. That's the Universe's way of saying it wants you to carry on.

You can probably think of a time in your life when you were doing something you loved so much, it gave you an influx of energy that just carried you effortlessly. But when you're doing something that doesn't excite you, you feel flat and uninspired; that's Life's way of telling you that you're not meant to be doing that thing.

Use your engine on the right things

You are hyper-capable; it's just the way you were built so you could live out this multi-passionate life. But just because you *can* do everything, it doesn't mean you *should* do everything, especially doing everything for everyone else. You're meant to fill your plate up with things you enjoy, not just anything at all. It's actually better to say no to some things and temporarily have less going on, because that will leave room for more of the things you *do* want to come in. There's a huge difference between having a full plate of things that feed you and filling your plate for the sake of it.

So, Manifesting Generator, give yourself the permission to have the most unrealistically good, full life. Because that's what you came here to show us.

Projector

A Projector has an undefined Sacral center and neither the Heart, Emotions, nor Root connected to the Throat by a full colored channel.

The Essence of a Projector

A Projector has the gift of seeing things in a way that others can't

You are here to tweak, improve, and make things more efficient in the specific ways that only you are able to do. Whether that's reading into people, devising systems, or designing new ways of doing things, each Projector has a special ability(s) of their own.

It's like being a bird up on a branch – you can see the lions and zebras trying to go from A to B, and because you have a vantage point, you can guide them to get to where they want to go in a better, more efficient way. You have the ability to gain a higher perspective and total clarity about certain specific parts of life, and your Purpose is to use that to improve and refine the way others do things.

When your efforts are focused on guiding and making improvements is when you will be your most successful and fulfilled.

You will be valued for what you see rather than what you do

Success comes from you sharing your insight with the world. The first step is to accept that your 'work' looks different from the rest of the world's work. It's about *seeing* – and not just doing, doing, doing. People won't value you based on how much you work, they'll value you based on how much you're adding to their lives. You're here to show, present, teach, consult, or guide others toward a new or better way, no matter what your actual job title is.

All Projectors are experts at understanding systems and how they could work better. All Projectors have specific areas or subjects that they see so clearly – those are the subjects they are meant to focus on and get so good at. If you're trying to figure out what those are, it's easy – they're the subjects that absolutely fascinate you. The Universe made them fascinating to you specifically because they are tied to your Purpose. Follow the areas of life you could learn about or talk about all day – those are the areas you are meant to apply your seeing gifts to. Your fascinations are not random; they are Divine.

The Role of a Projector

You are here to help us work and function better – and it starts with you

Your system is built very efficiently so you can get done in three hours what we've been taught takes us eight. You've been taught that overworking makes you important and successful, but you will always feel depleted and unsatisfied if you fall into this belief; you can end up putting so much energy into something and not getting that much in return. You can have some level of success but still feel, deep down, that there is an easier way.

You are here to unchain yourself from this obsession with productivity that we've all been conditioned with, so that you can be a master at making the rest of the world more harmonious and efficient.

The more you're helping improve the way we live and work, the more successful you become. This is the formula you can rely on and bring yourself back to whenever you're trying to create your next level in life.

Projector Energy Patterns

Your battery may be smaller, but it's more efficient

Your energy level is perfectly built to help you with your Purpose. Instead of being built to just output all day long, you are built to spend most of your time observing, learning, processing, refining, and developing your genius. The newness and innovation that comes when you do this is your highest value-add to the world – so this is an investment. For this reason, Life will require you to rest more often than you might have been told is 'normal' or necessary for a successful life.

You only need to share and output when there really is a need for it – and when there really is a need, it will go a long way. You can be sharing all day when there isn't a need, and it won't bring anyone any benefit. Pressuring yourself to keep up with others who you deem to be more powered up than you will only exhaust you and keep you out of your genius, which happens in the observing and processing times. And when your seeing is on point, not only will more people recognize

Projector

The day you recognize yourself
is the day others will start
to recognize you too.

it in you, but, when it comes to sharing it, it will bring so much value and take you so much further.

Trust that whatever your skills and gifts are, the Universe placed them in you for a reason – to make the world a better place. So just because your seeing comes easy to you, don't ever doubt that it is worth its weight in gold when you share it.

How to Get Aligned as a Projector

Only share your gifts with people who want to receive them

Deep down, you know you have valuable advice and guidance that could help people – and you've possibly felt this way since you were a child. However, you've probably also been at a time in your life when you've given someone advice you knew was valuable, but felt it was unwelcome. When someone doesn't have a desire or interest in what you have to share, anything you say will literally *bounce* right off their energy instead of sinking in – so you may think you are helping, but if they're not open, it won't land. If you keep trying to get certain people to 'get it,' you will only deplete your own energy. Focus on sharing your guidance with the people who actually want what you've got, because those will reap rewards effortlessly.

Make yourself available

Creating a successful career won't come from pushing and forcing. If you ever try to make stuff happen by reaching out, giving unsolicited advice, telling people what to do, or controlling the circumstances – you'll only come up against difficulty, resistance, and blocks. Instead, you want to use your energy to create a format for your gifts so that people can easily see and understand them – that way the right people who want them will come to you and ask for them. Doing things this way will make success easy and effortless.

Whenever you're feeling stuck, ask yourself: 'What can I do to make myself more available?' Recognizing your own gifts and valuing them yourself is the first step to other people seeing them too. Think about your energy field as your billboard – when you are clear on your contribution and the value it has, it will advertise you correctly no matter where you are (whether that's in the grocery store, at work, or online). It's all the same as far as the Universe is concerned.

Reflector

A Reflector has all of their nine centers undefined (white).

The Essence of a Reflector

Reflectors pick up on everything

When you look at a Reflector's chart, you'll see it's unusually white and open, which is rare – only 1 percent of the population has this. This openness means you are radically receptive to the world around you and its energies – you take it all on.

This means your Essence is very clear, like a blank canvas that's constantly experiencing what it's like to be different paintings depending on what's being 'painted on' that day. There are two distinct sources of paint.

1. **The energies of the people and places you are in.**

   Your energy is like a disco ball – if there's even one small beam of light in the room, the disco ball will amplify it to the max. If something is happening around you that's at a one out of 10, you can feel it with the intensity of an eight out of 10. Because of this, you pick up on energies that are just too subtle for others, and you can use them as the gifts they are to inform everything you do.

   You can be high-energy sometimes, lower the next, highly emotional sometimes, and extremely unemotional the next – depending on what you're taking in from around you. Sometimes you might wonder which one is 'you' – but the answer is, you are it all, just none of it consistently. You are here to experience life in a much more full and varied way than other people, and that's actually what your Soul craves.

2. **The energies in the cosmos at the time.**

   Even if you weren't taking in energy from people or places, the world goes through energy 'weather' that changes every day. Each day is a progression of the previous day, and together they create cycles of energy that lead us to evolution. So for example, there are learning days and doing days; emotional days and more dispassionate days. We all need to experience this range of energy, but because you are Reflecting it, you can feel (and tap into) it more deeply. They say Reflectors are Lunar beings, because, to help us, they are able to identify the different, predictable cycles of energy that the moon's cycle is shining down on us.

It's important you know this process of picking up on everything is not controlled by the mind, it's just a mechanical function of your aura. So it's not like you're choosing when to do this and when to not. All this information is coming to you anyway; you can use it to your advantage by becoming aware of what's coming at you, and familiarizing yourself with what it's saying.

Reflectors are the ultimate chameleons

Being so open energetically also makes you very prone to outside conditioning – the voices that say you need to be a certain fixed way to be loved, successful, and happy. This is the deepest myth that you came here to overcome. There is no one quality you 'have' to consistently be to get what you want. The magic is in being open to changing and shifting at any point you feel pulled into – and not identify with it. Just experience it, feel it, and witness it. Let it pass through you like a teacher and gift giver.

Your Radical Openness can either be a weakness or a superpower. It all depends on if you allow your vibe to be what your Soul genuinely leads you to be on that day, or if you're letting your conditioning dictate how to be, feel, and think.

The fact that you want to be one thing one day and another thing the next is a GOOD thing – and on a soul level, you actually crave a wide, varied existence. Not everyone has that ability. That's your power move and, thus, also what people will actually value in you the most. You just have to be brave enough to try it before anyone tells you it will pay off.

The Role of a Reflector

You are a mirror who can show the rest of us who we really are

When a Reflector allows their persona to change and flow according to who and what is around it, then a Reflector is able to do what it came here to do; to be clear enough to mirror the vibe of the other. This is where the name Reflector comes from: when we're around a clear Reflector, it shows us exactly what we are. This benefits both you and the other person.

You're a clean slate, and when people interact with you, they see what they project out on you reflected right back at them. This is such a valuable tool for humanity. In Human Design we say that a Reflector belongs at the center of a community so that everyone in that community has a way of doing some self-examination. There's a spiritual theory that says what you see in another is simply parts of yourself that you don't see. This is true to some extent for all people, but it is REALLY crystal clear and unfiltered when people look at a Reflector who is free and unattached from needing to always be a certain way. It's way more fun for your Soul to shape-shift and embody so many different energies depending on where life takes you rather than to stay fixed and stuck.

You can do anything you like with your life; as long as you get your energy clear and open wherever you go, you will be fulfilling your Purpose. When that's your intention, anything you put your efforts into will soar.

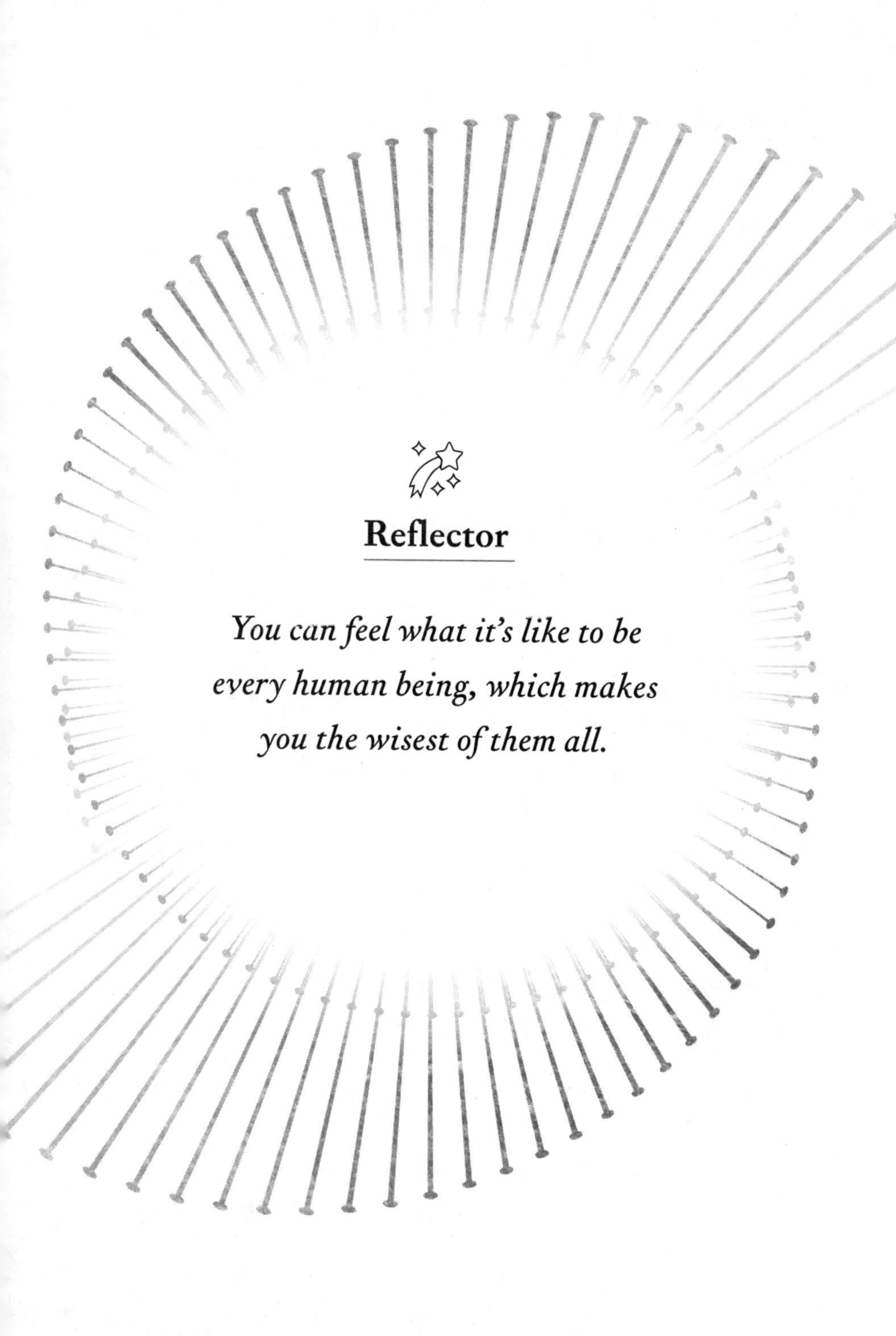

Reflector

You can feel what it's like to be every human being, which makes you the wisest of them all.

Reflector Energy Patterns

Mastering your specific energy pattern

You don't have a set energy level – it will ebb and flow, and it will also mirror whatever environment you're in. If you need a burst of energy in order to accomplish something, surround yourself with productive and energetic people or environments and that will make you feel like the most turbocharged of them all. However, you can't do this consistently because nothing about you is meant to be consistent, and you'll eventually burn out if you act like the rest of the world on a regular basis.

This is because you didn't come here to be high-energy all the time; contrary to what we've been told, this won't lead to success for you, and it will actually deplete you and burn you out if you're constantly trying to go full power because you think that's how you have to be.

Think of yourself as a power socket; if you put too much electricity in, you'll blow a fuse. But if you pay attention to how much you can handle that day, be really smart about what you use that energy to accomplish that actually moves you toward your goals and dreams, and then pull away and reset, that's your magic formula. It's not about doing the most, it's about doing the few things that will reward you the most.

How to Get Aligned as a Reflector

Curate your environment

The Universe will always use your environment to show you what's Aligned and not Aligned for you. If you feel good in a place, that's how you know you're in the right place at the right time. If you don't feel good, that's not what it intends for you right now. It's time to move.

In terms of work, you can take on whatever work role you enjoy. The sign that you're in a job that's Aligned for you is if you feel good in your work environment(s). If you're in a job where you feel good in some environments and not in others, it's a sign to step out of or change the ones you don't enjoy.

Success for a Reflector comes from the commitment to leaving places where you don't feel good, and bringing in more of the environments, groups and situations where you do. When you string moments of right place, right time together, and let them add up, it creates a life of effortless success and happiness because what you're doing is lining up with all the synchronicities and opportunities that the Universe is waiting to send your way. You don't have to go out and actively 'grab' any of it, you just have to get Aligned with it, so that it comes to you. You can use your openness to your advantage by 'plugging in' to places and people that feel good to you – that's always how you'll know what's Aligned.

Detach yourself from labels and the need to describe yourself

Reflectors LIVE for feeling like life is constantly surprising and delighting them. But any time you label yourself, that puts you in a box, which blocks that feeling of surprise. Your great work as a Reflector is to let go of any label or method by which you define or describe yourself and leave it open to changing. Be malleable and flexible. That is the most magnetic state a Reflector can be in.

Approaching whatever your passions are in this world with that malleable openness will help you be your most successful – because the people and opportunities already swirling around you will be attracted to you most when you are that way.

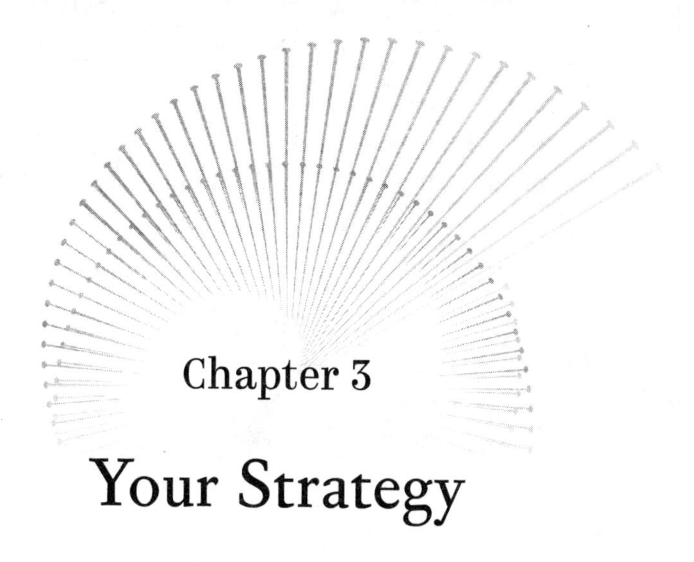

Chapter 3

Your Strategy

Your Strategy describes the best way for you to make something happen in your life, whether big or small.

There are so many experts out there telling you how to create success, and maybe you've tried to do it the way they said, but it didn't help much, and then you wound up thinking there was something wrong with *you*.

In reality you were just using a method that wasn't a fit for your authentic Essence.

The world has taught us we have to push and force to make things happen. But when you go about Life in the way that suits your energy, doors open, flow happens, things come together with less efforting. This is Alignment.

When you're not true to your Essence, it will always create extra resistance on your path. For example, things will come to you with more difficulty or won't happen at all, even if you're trying so hard – because you're trying to be like someone you're not.

How do you know doing things your way works?

Like everything else, it's experiential. When you do your part and try showing up as you, expect the Universe to do *its* part and come through for you so that you know this is right. And when you know it works, when you see the results in your life, it becomes easier and easier to do.

Remember the Universe just wants you to be more you, so it's incentivized to give you encouragement and ease when you do so.

There's a lot of talk about manifesting things into reality – and in spiritual circles, they talk about getting your intentions right. But actions are necessary too. Not the type where you push and force – the type where your actions are You painting your intentions onto the canvas of Life. Your Strategy tells you the best and most effective way to paint so you get the most bang for your buck out of every action taken. You minimize wasted energy and efforts because you're aiming your bows correctly and on target.

Everything you want is already meant to come to you – those things are swirling around your aura, your energy body, waiting to come in. All that ever happens when you manifested something in the past is that you stepped up to the next level of who you're capable of being in some way, which now means you have a bigger aura – which now holds that bigger level of your life. So it drops in.

Informing

The Strategy of a Manifestor

You're not meant to try to 'make' things happen. You're meant to go off and do your own thing, which doesn't involve asking anyone else's permission for anything.

Trust that your urges will kick off a chain reaction in other people who see what you're up to, but that you don't and shouldn't think about the side effects when you do your thing. Create what you're called to create, do and say what's trying to come out of you. But remember that whatever it is you're up to, there are gonna be people who want to get on your train. And in order for the right people to be magnetized to you, all you have to do is openly share what you're doing, thinking, working on, considering. This is informing: you activate a sorting mechanism that ensures all the right parts come together without you really having to 'make' it come together. All the perfect circumstances will unfold, but you have to bring people's attention to what you're starting. In terms of energy, what you do is the 'cause' that everyone else reacts to, which creates 'effects.'

All you have to do is inform

Now this may sound easy enough, but for a Manifestor, unapologetically sharing without shrinking is challenging. The world conditions you to believe you *shouldn't* be doing that, so a lot of the times, you have a tendency to hesitate or err on the side of discretion. Or you just want to go off and do your thing in silence, because then you won't encounter questioning, resistance, interference, judgment, or criticism.

Being seen is scary for you because you equate it with all these things, which are super limiting and constricting to your Spirit.

But there's another way

It's your energy that actually dictates how the sharing openly is received. When a Manifestor is totally accepting of their true nature and urges (because at the end of the day, the Universe gave them to you), then shares them without needing the acceptance from the outside world, ironically, people accept it more because they're responding to your energy around it – and the right people will even adore it.

However, when you are avoiding informing, people pick up on that, and they will actually end up *doing* the poking, prodding, and judging, etc. – which then confirms your fear and makes you want to keep hiding. Every time you make incremental changes toward being totally open with people, you will be better received. And all of a sudden, people who seemed maybe totally uninterested will want to know more. You will pique the interest of strangers. And people will come out of seemingly nowhere to help support you and bring momentum to whatever it is you're starting.

Know that being unapologetic doesn't have to be loud or aggressive or shoving it down other people's throats. The best way for you to share is in whatever way feels authentic and genuine to you. Being unapologetic just means you being totally happy with it in yourself and not offering it up to others for their approval. When you share it from the heart, without needing a certain response from it, you are free. And when you are free, your actions will create ripples that affect people in the best ways possible. People want to follow free, big, unapologetic people, and this is what you really are.

Responding

The Strategy of Generators and Manifesting Generators

The Universe is constantly sending you clues and signs of the next right thing based on what excites you, what Lights you up, and what doesn't. Responding is about only doing things that come across your path that you can literally feel a full-body yes to. When something is meant for you, your Gut will literally respond to it – you will feel physically drawn to that thing.

Think of life as one big buffet: it's full of ideas and suggestions and options that might please you. Responding is noticing all the things you see and come across that make you think 'I like that,' 'I want that,' or 'I wish I could have that.' And if you do like it and want it – say yes to it, go do it, create it for yourself, bring more of it into your life, because doing it is what the Universe wants you to do next. These could be direct things, like opportunities and invitations that come your way, or indirect, like things you see around you, things you see other people doing, what you see on social media, characters on TV shows. They are all there on purpose to lead you right to your Purpose.

The answers are all around you

You don't have to 'figure out what you want'; the outside world will prompt you to ask if you're into whatever's in front of you or not.

So don't pressure yourself to just 'know what you want' out of thin air; you have to have an outside stimulus to respond to.

You don't have to push, force, or 'make it happen': you just have to fully throw your energy into things, but only once your Gut has given you the go-ahead. If you haven't gotten a 'hell yes!' from your Gut, it's probably a no.

When you are open, the Universe will put the things that are meant for you right in front of your eyes.

Your decisions are black and white

It's important for you to know that the Gut is black and white – it doesn't do gray areas. So, for you, you're either excited about it or you're not. Unless you feel a full-body yes, the answer is actually no. You don't deal in maybes.

Because the Gut is black and white, it also doesn't deal in open-ended questions. So, if you ask yourself, 'What Lights me up?' don't be surprised if your Gut hasn't come up with the answer. But if you ask yourself, 'Does forecasting light me up?' 'Does event planning light me up?' 'Does organization light me up?' – you'll definitely know the answer.

You can use this-or-that and yes-or-no questions to direct you with literally anything too. So, instead of asking yourself what takeout you feel like for dinner tonight, ask yourself if you want sushi or Mexican food. The more you can make sure that everything in your life is there because it gives you that 'hell yes!' response, the more Aligned you become. The Universe makes you respond yes to the things it wants you to do. And it doesn't see the difference between you saying yes to the takeout that Lights you up and yes to the job that Lights you up. Following your lit-up-ness always creates more lit-up-ness.

What to do when it feels like life isn't sending you things to respond to

The more you get rid of things that don't light you up, the more space you will have to notice new things that might; it's like you give yourself a bigger pair of glasses with which to see.

Take a look around your life and ask if each thing in it Lights you up or not. If it doesn't, that's okay – start by just being honest with yourself about it, as that will align you with the truth of how you feel, and from there, the Universe is clear on your feelings so it can swoop in and start to guide you, give you strength, and help you by putting new opportunities and clues on your path.

And then start to look around at whatever else is going on in the world around you and keep asking your Gut, 'Would this be exciting to you if you had it?' And then pursue those wants. Put energy into bringing them into your own life. If you got a 'hell yes,' you have full permission to funnel all your Life Force into it. Always trust the feeling of wanting as a good thing, because it's pointing you toward the Life you're supposed to have.

Being Invited

The Strategy of a Projector

You're here to guide people toward good or better way(s) of doing and being in the specific ways that only you can see. But first, you have to make sure that the people you're about to share your guidance with actually want to hear it or receive it. You've probably given unsolicited advice before and found that it doesn't lead to good things on either side; maybe people shut you out, call you bossy, or you're left feeling unappreciated, unheard, or undervalued. You wonder why other people just don't 'get it.' You're probably aware that you know things or see things a certain way that could help other people, and it's normal to want to share those things. But not everybody wants to hear or is ready to hear it, and it's not your job to make them. If you are here right now, there are plenty of people who do want to benefit from you guiding them. Save it for those people and places, because there, it will reap the most benefit – and you'll feel more confident in the quality of your guidance, which will make it easier to keep doing.

In order for people to invite you, you just have to turn your light on so those who want it can see it before they ask for it. Get clear on what it is that you see so well that others don't, what specific take you have on something existing, or what niche subject you understand so clearly that others don't. What's your specific value-add that you can make to life? And then own it – this turns your light on in your aura, because your aura is advertising what you're capable of.

Being invited can be as overt as an offer or request for your services. It can also be more subtle, like someone asking a question where, underneath, you can sense the tone of being interested, but maybe they're too shy to ask you outright. Either way, an invitation is when a person sees what you have to offer and genuinely wants to receive it.

The number of invitations you receive is directly correlated to:

1. **How much you recognize and own the value of what you bring to the table**

   Others can't recognize you 'know things' unless you emit the vibe of a person who is secure in their gifts. Let's say you're an artist, and you want people to buy your art. You have to create your art first for people to see and then buy it – or at least have examples of what your art looks like. The same goes for being at the very beginning of a business; say you want to be a health and wellness expert – start sharing your tips on Instagram to arouse people's interest. If this is an Aligned career for you, and you're bringing forth a new take on it, people will start asking you questions or wanting advice. This is an invitation.

2. **How available you're making your gifts**

   You'll want to have a clear format you present to others about what you do. Have a structure or container for the advice you're offering – whether that's a list of services, a one-on-one session, courses, or creations. Or if you're applying for a job, make sure your résumé communicates what you actually want to bring to the table rather than what you think it needs to say for you to get the role.

When you have open channels that people can receive your gifts and skills through, it's clear to them what they could get, so there's a possibility of them asking you for them.

Being Carried

The Strategy of a Reflector

Because you are spontaneous and open, you make your dreams happen in very different ways than other human beings. A lot of the time, life is actually *carrying* you more than directing you like it does to the other types. And it's carrying you right to your dreams if you just get out of the way. That is, getting rid of the things you think you have to do or should do and seeing what the Universe keeps nudging you toward.

You will know that something is right when the Universe repeatedly nudges you to do it. Go back to those Lunar cycles – you want to make sure something feels right in every phase of 'You' that you go through before doing it – especially if it's a big thing. If there's something you're meant to do, it will *keep* coming to you, almost like it won't leave you alone, and like it's coming from outside of you. When that happens, you can throw your full energy into doing what it says.

But resist the urge to act on anything at the first nudge. You have no way of telling if it's right unless you have allowed it to play out over time a little bit. And you have no idea if it's even your nudge the first time – since you're so open you could be picking up on what someone else around you could or should be doing. But when things keep repeating, you know you can trust them. With time, you'll also find that the nudges paint the picture for you more and more so you can see them very clearly in your mind's eye, which will make them come to life so much more easily.

It's good to wait

The world will pressure you to act straight away, but if you rush your timeline, you won't be aligning with Divine Timing. Imagine if you sent someone that email today, it might not be the perfect time for them to receive it, but in two-week's time, once you've let your nudges play out, they respond perfectly. Or if you rush to form a company now, but later, once the nudges have developed, a better way of structuring it would come to you. This is the power of waiting.

When you are totally sure of something because *Life* has kept putting it at your door, not because you've 'shoulded' yourself into thinking you want to do it, your energy is Aligned. And whenever we act from a place of Alignment is when things easily fall into place without much effort from your behalf. This is you being carried.

When you don't wait

If you've ever created something or worked toward something that you acted on prematurely, it's likely you experienced unnecessary delays or diversions.

Whereas, if you wait until you literally feel pushed to do it, everything comes together much more easily and just 'happens.'

This is the way you are built for. Life will always show you the way, quite literally, if you stay open to doing whatever it nudges you to do.

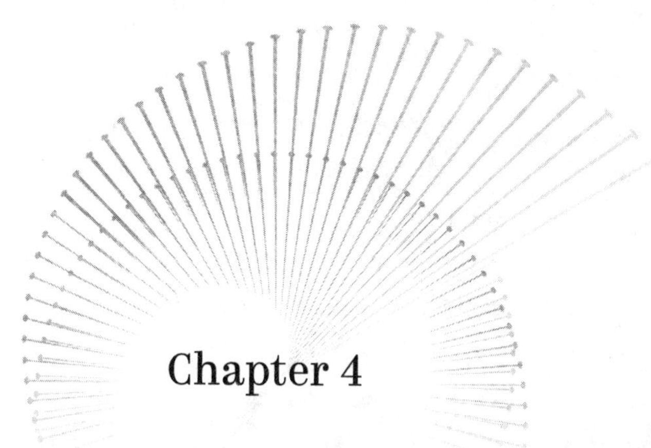

Chapter 4

Your Signature and Not-Self

Inside your system, there is a mechanism that can always show you where you're Aligned and where you're not.

Each Energy Type has a specific sign it gets when it's doing something that's in line with its truest, best expression, and a sign when it's doing the opposite. These are called the Signature and the Not-Self.

When you're using your energy correctly, you will feel your Signature come up, and it's a no-fail way to know you're on the right track. So you never have to do any guesswork to know whether you're in Alignment or not – you will get that confirmation.

And similarly, the Universe also sends you a sign when you're doing something that's not for you.

The Not-Self is basically a term for the feeling that comes whenever you're being or thinking in a way that isn't your best self. Not being yourself = Not-Self.

Life gives you this feeling to make it easy to spot when you're getting off track so that you can redirect quickly back to using your energy the way you're meant to.

So wherever you're at in your life, in small moments and big moments, you can tell if you're on the path based on which one is present – your Signature or your Not-Self.

Our entire lives will be a mixture of our Signature and our Not-Self, because Life is always going to have your back and show you what's right for you and what's not, no matter how high you go in your journey, there will always be higher heights it can bring you to. You will always have aspects of your Not-Self to transform.

It's not that you always feel one and not the other, it's not all-or-nothing like that. You'll meander between both, but the more Aligned you get, the more time you'll spend in your Signature and less in your Not-Self. Often you feel different ones in different areas of your life.

Try not to shame yourself when you feel your Not-Self come up, because shame is what will prevent you from noticing and admitting the Not-Self when it does come up. The Not-Self *wants* to be seen because that's the way the Universe is trying to get through to you to show you the exact, perfect next thing to work on. The Not-Self is not *you* – it's just a feeling that visits to guide you.

It's ironic that the more Aligned you get, the stronger and more jarring you'll feel your Not-Self when it does comes up, because it won't be your norm anymore. When you're out of Alignment and it feels yucky – congratulate yourself for feeling so yucked by it, because it means you so deeply feel how wrong it is for you now. You're fully awake to its ill-fittingness as opposed to being so asleep to it that you can't tell what's what.

Manifestor

The Signature of a Manifestor Is Peace

When you're doing what YOU truly want to do, fully trusting and relying on your True Self, you feel at Peace – with no one bothering you, no one pressuring you to be or do anything you don't want to, no one expecting you to fit into a certain thing. But most importantly, you aren't putting any pressures or expectations on yourself, just recognizing that all you need to do is keep doing what your Divine, spontaneous nature urges you to do. Although they are here to create movement(s), Manifestors don't want to rule from on high, they don't want to micromanage people, they don't want to have a million people to answer to – they want to be left alone and have the freedom to do whatever they feel like doing next.

When you've let go of needing to know what to do in order to get your dream life and instead trust that your inner urges will lead you right to it, you will feel that inner Peace and space to breathe and play that you so crave. You can blast off as many times as you want with no limitations on you and also let it all go in between those bursts of energy and come back to total nothingness. Life seems like your blank canvas, full of promise, all over again.

The Not-Self of a Manifestor Is Anger

We feel Anger whenever we feel that we've been wronged by someone else. Since a Manifestor's challenge is about being in their power, the opposite of that is someone else having power or control over them. You may have been conditioned to believe that being in your power makes you bad, unacceptable, or dangerous, or you're afraid of it, so unconsciously seek to place other people in positions of control or on pedestals in your life. It's also easier for a Manifestor to believe that their situation is other people's doing because then, at least, you can blame them – there is someone else to be mad at. For as long as you are not giving yourself full permission to do things the way you want to do them, without looking for the okay from others, you will always be angry or mad at something or someone.

When you feel angry, it's always your cue to be your own permission slip and do what your Soul truly craves to do in this moment, what is most important to you. You might be afraid to do this because you're afraid to make a mistake, which would mean that you'd then be mad at yourself. But know that if you are living your Design, you will always receive the right guidance on what to do. If you do occasionally make choices that are not Soul choices, that's part of your learning to come back to yourself. This is where you need to practice knowing that just because you made 'bad' choices doesn't equate with being a 'bad' person. Accepting yourself and having your own back when you need it is what will dissolve that Anger into Peace. Anger doesn't necessarily mean raging and screaming, it's an internal feeling like things are not right or not fair.

Anger can feel like:

- 'Why can everyone else do that, and I can't?'
- 'The rules are different for everyone else.'
- Holding on to tension.

- You're at the mercy of other people's agendas.
- You have no control over your own life.
- You're bending, bending, bending all the time and that you're about to snap.
- You're mad or annoyed at people for having done things 'to' you.
- Things are bubbling under the surface, and maybe you feel it or maybe you're trying to stuff it down or ignore it, because it's 'bad' to be anything but placating and sweet.
- Being caged.
- You can't see straight (and maybe that other people can) or are starting to doubt your own abilities and visions.
- Constantly questioning yourself ('What am I not seeing?').

That feeling of Anger comes from deeply doubting yourself and then believing that there's something wrong with you that's leading to your lack of being where you want to be. There is nothing fundamentally wrong with you. You are destined for greatness and happiness like everyone else. You just have to be okay with doing it your way and knowing that that's the way the Universe wants you to do it.

When you are so happy and trusting in your always being able to do what your Soul is calling you to do and couldn't care less about outside factors, you will always revert back into your Sign of Peace. This is where you belong.

Generators and Manifesting Generators

The Signature of Generators and Manifesting Generators Is Satisfaction

Satisfaction is feeling Lit up by Life. That feeling you get when something is pleasing to you – is how you know you're Aligned. It really is as simple as pleasure. This could be anything you really savor like your perfect coffee in the morning, the buzz in your work life, a warm cuddle with your loved ones, the tennis game that makes you feel so alive, and the good kind of crazy days that make you feel invigorated. When you string these moments together where you feel so content in each, you get to the end of your day and can't help but let out a good kind of satisfied sigh. Satisfaction comes from letting yourself enjoy your life and not just getting through it. It comes from you filling your life with things you love and then fully drinking in all the pleasure they have to give you.

The Not-Self of Generators and Manifesting Generators Is Frustration

If you're living your Design, saying yes to things that light you up and no to the things that don't, you create a steady flow of excitement in your life, which then magnetizes people and opportunities to you. The opposite of energy flowing is energy stagnating. This creates a feeling of being stuck and not being able to move things forward even if you try. This is the true definition of Frustration: attempting or reaching for something, but it not happening. Frustration can show up as literal Frustration or irritation, feeling stuck, feeling uninspired, blah, or incapable. This is always a sign showing you that you have the power to change your situation by changing one of your thoughts or behaviors around the situation.

How Frustration can look in your thoughts:

- Nothing is happening.
- This is not going the way I want.
- I'm so bored.
- I'm so over this.
- I'm being made/forced to do this, but I don't want to.
- I have all these obligations, and they're starting to weigh heavy on me. I want to shake them off and be free.
- I feel like I'm having the life sucked out of me.
- I'm being pulled in all these different directions.
- It seems like everyone else is doing what they love, but nothing is coming to me/I can't seem to do that.
- I should be able to create happiness, but I just can't.
- I have no energy to do what I dream of.
- What's the point of all of this?
- Why does it feel like walking through mud and taking so much effort to get things going?
- I'm so tired.

Remember that this is not your TRUE self – this is your Not-Self, a.k.a. Life showing you that it's time to live your Design a little bit more, which will get you right back into your Signature. You are here to be Lit up and excited by life. This is your real Nature, and whenever you see your Not-Self, you can rise higher into the life you really want to have by turning it around. Use your Frustration as a cue to change something up that can lead you back to an outcome that would make you feel the most satisfied.

Projector

The Signature of a Projector Is Success

Because your Purpose is to improve the way we live, in your own unique way – when you're doing that, there is no way you can't be brought Success in your outside world – because the more value you're providing to the world, the more the Universe will place you in a position where you can continue to guide and serve in an even bigger way.

Projectors are often obsessed with Success and being successful – but that is your Soul telling you that you know that's where you need to be. Don't ever judge your desire to be successful. Sure, there is a negative way this can look – believing it makes us better than others, believing there's not enough of it to go round, believing you have to take it from others. But there is also a positive way this can look – wanting Success because for you that's fun and makes you feel like you're living life to the fullest more than anything else will. When you are focusing on providing true value to other people's processes – Success will effortlessly follow.

The Not-Self of a Projector Is Bitterness

Because Projectors are built to improve things, they easily spot all that needs improvement. Seeing all that is wrong with the world can create Bitterness if we sit on it instead of turning it into wisdom and learning.

Bitterness can show up as irritation or judgment over others, spending too much time focusing on what's wrong, harboring even low-grade resentment, whether at specific people or at life or the world in general.

Noticing something negative is good when it can prompt you to come up with an improvement. But it will drain your energy levels, enjoyment of life, and success when you spend too much time dwelling on it. If you take the intel it has to offer you, and then move on, you can use it to redirect yourself right back to success.

How this can sound in your thoughts:

- Feeling jealous over other people's success.
- Well, eff them, I don't need them or like them anyway.
- They should be doing it this way.
- They're 'not getting it,' or they're dumb.
- A screw you/screw that kind of mentality.
- Thinking over and over about other people's faults and shortcomings.
- Thinking about what you or others 'should' be doing instead.

All these kinds of thoughts are your conditioned thoughts, which are not the real you. When you indulge in them, they literally pull you out of your lane, because it's you using your seeing gifts the wrong way – seeing with the need to feed your insecurities rather than from a neutral place where you can use them to serve and give. You're living your Purpose when you're bringing improvements to the world in the way you're designed to. The Bitterness can creep up when you're focusing too much on other stuff, including:

- All the things that displease you about life.
- All the things that feel wrong.
- All the things you can't change, or control, and shouldn't be concerning yourself with.
- Things you think you can't change, but that you actually can.

Reflector

The Signature of a Reflector Is Surprise

What Reflectors crave more than anything is to feel delighted by life, in awe of all it has to offer. This is the feeling of Surprise. Reflectors don't want to feel like life is predictable and humdrum; they want to feel like – 'I wonder what life has in store for me?' So when you're living your Design, you deeply feel in reverence of how wonderful life is and can be.

You do this by allowing yourself to be fluid and open. For example, be super regimented at work one day when you feel like it and then have a more relaxed attitude the next – not judging one as a better way but letting yourself see how cool and fun each of those vibes is. Running on a treadmill until it stops being enjoyable and then switching to yoga without attaching any logic, story, or justification to it. Bask in it all and let it change as often as it wants to.

Of course, there will be certain things you're more into and certain things in life that don't appeal to you at all, but what's important is that you always feel like you have freedom and flexibility. You need to remember that life is full of options that it made just to tickle and delight you, and you can live in constant wonderment when you keep your eyes open to all these options. The less you lock yourself into one identity the better your life will flow. To you there's no better feeling than feeling how incredible and limitless and colorful life can be.

You love to be surprised by what life can send you, and when you feel surprised, that's how you know you're on the right track.

The Not-Self of a Reflector Is Disappointment

When you're not living your Design, and the surprise element of life gets sucked out of it, all that's left is the banal and the mundane. Imagine, you're meant to be experiencing the full rainbow spectrum of colors but all you see in your Not-Self is gray. Life begins to feel dull.

Here's how this can look in your thoughts:

- feeling blue
- feeling caged in or restricted

- feeling like life is meant to be so much more than this
- feeling let down by how other people are
- feeling disappointed by human beings in general
- feeling even low-grade depression
- feeling like other people have a much better life than you
- feeling like you're not living life to the full

Disappointment could also show up as a compulsive need to go overboard and cram as much life, routines, or experiences into this one life as possible.

Use Disappointment as a cue that something is off

It's wonderful to want to make the most out of your life, but you know the difference when it's driven by lack and control. Disappointment is always a cue for you to bust out of the frames you've boxed yourself into (whether that's a routine, a perception of self, a habit, an addiction) and be more fluid. Explore different fancies you haven't yet explored; for example, if your wardrobe is all neutrals, but one day you feel like wearing baby-blue, follow that urge. Bust out of the limits and narratives you've put on yourself, specifically any that are tied into the situation that has caused this feeling of Disappointment, and you'll start to feel life in living color again.

Chapter 5

Your Authority

Your Authority is the part that's in charge of making your life decisions – listening to it always shows you what the right Aligned choice is. Imagine if you never had to stress about the right decision because you could always rely on an in-built mechanism to tell you. This is how simple and clear it's meant to be.

Right now, we spend so much time agonizing over what we should do next, feeling torn between what to do, what choice to make. This is because we've been told to make decisions from our minds – so we try to 'be smart' and know the outcomes of all options before we choose. This leads us to try to figure out the end results, except there's no way any human being knows what can unfold. What ensues are feelings of control, helplessness, clinging, and fear. We are not meant to know what's coming next – we are meant to make the Aligned choice that's presenting itself to us today, which automatically starts our tomorrow at the next level up in this game called Life. Choosing the things and actions the real you would take is the ultimate 'control' because it always guarantees you the best outcome without you ever needing to know what the outcome is. Hence, there is room for it to be better than what your brain could have conceived.

Your Authority is the voice of your specific Intuition, and it lives and speaks through your BODY not your mind. Everyone has a different part of their body in charge of their decision-making so their minds can be free to focus on the outside world and develop their genius. Getting to know your specific Authority helps dissipate those lost or confused feelings in your life and ensures you'll be in your magic lane (the fast track to living your dream life) quicker than you can imagine.

- When your Authority is Emotional, your Intuition speaks to you through how you feel about something.
- When your Authority is Sacral, your Intuition speaks to you through your Gut.
- When your Authority is Splenic, your Intuition speaks to you through your instincts, or sixth sense.
- When you have Ego Authority, your Intuition speaks to you through your wants.
- When you have G Center Authority, your Intuition comes when you put pen to paper or talk it out.
- When you have Mental Authority, your Intuition gives you this feeling of 'It just makes sense to me.'
- When you have Lunar Authority, you don't have to come up with the right answer inside – Life will reveal the right choices to you if you sit back and let them come at the perfect time.

Even if, in the moment you hear your Authority, you're not ready to act on it, simply listen and acknowledge the message – this will ensure that your Authority will continue to speak to you and get louder over time.

Also, you don't have to trust it overnight – test it out on the small things first, build up evidence, see how it supports you in your real life. Then, and only then, will you be able to trust it unconditionally.

Emotional Authority

How You Feel About It

When your Authority is Emotional, it means your emotions are the CEO of your aura and life.

It means that the right choice for you is always the one that makes you feel happy or content when you think about it.

Your emotions toward something, toward *any* choice, are not random; they are the way the Universe specifically tells *you* the right way to go in any situation in your life, and you can always rely on them to show you what the most Aligned option is.

Because you're an emotional being, you have to give your body time to fully feel out the situation or opportunity in order to give you the answer. Say you're having a day where you feel on top of the world: this feeling will override everything, and, through the rose-colored glasses, anything that comes your way will look like a more attractive prospect. The same goes with a low day – it will skew your decisions equally. In order to *really* see how you feel about something, you need to wait out your emotion-colored glasses and then assess the opportunity from that neutral place.

Exploring this way of living is pretty radical because it means you shouldn't pressure yourself to have the answer right away. It's such a departure from what we're taught, which is that you should respond to emails right as they come up, that it's good if you always have a perfect comeback, that you need to tell people if you're in or out on the spot. If you try to do that, you will cut yourself off from so much knowledge and wisdom that gets gathered up by your body when you just give yourself a little bit of time.

Neutral places are for making decisions and getting clarity. Emotional highs and lows are the birthplace of creativity, of inspiration, of ideas, of experiencing what it is to be human. You live your whole life on what's called an Emotional wave – imagine the Universe is a DJ and you are the radio station: your job is not to choose the vibe; you are here to feel and transmit the songs. Getting rid of any judgment about the songs that are coming through for you at any given time is the greatest gift you can give yourself, and you can't even conceive of what they will create for you. You simply have to jump into the stream.

Listen to the feel-good

If something is good for you, big or small, it will evoke a sweet kind of emotion in your body just by your thinking about it. And if it makes you feel low or flat or sad or blue, even if it doesn't make sense to you why, then it's not Aligned for you. When you're just starting out listening to your emotions, don't pressure yourself to act on them right out of the gate; just acknowledging them is a huge step in reconnecting and strengthening your communication line with the Universe. And when you do, it will speak to you more clearly and loudly, and you will find it easier to follow. When you give your emotions the deciding vote, it eliminates so much of the confusion that dims our Knowing and makes it so difficult to trust ourselves.

Time shows you how you really feel about things – take it

Let's say something comes up that makes you super excited; you might want to jump in and say yes in the moment. But you can probably think of a time when you've been in a super good mood one day and said yes to something – only to wake up the next day and regret the decision.

Being in a good or bad mood one day can sway your clarity, so you need to wait until you're in that neutral mood. When you're in neutral, come back to the decision and see how it makes you feel. If it makes you smile in *that* state, then it's a good decision for sure.

Go slow to go fast

We've been taught that quick decisions and actions lead us to our dreams faster – but that's actually detrimental to you. By not jumping into commitments prematurely, you'll save yourself a lot of detours, which will also save you time. In your case, slower is definitely faster. So be okay with buying yourself time to get clarity; the more you do so and own it, the more you'll see that people are actually more okay with it than you thought.

You can try these kinds of phrases to give your emotions time to get clarity:

- 'Let me come back to you on that.'
- 'Let me sleep on it.'

- 'Give me 24 hours.' (Which, 80 percent of the time, is enough time for you to get clarity, but with bigger or more complex decisions it can take a bit longer than that. Trust that whenever it comes, that's Divine Timing at work.)

Trusting your feelings

Knowing how you feel emotionally can be a challenge at first because we're taught that emotions are unreliable, and that the head is better at being in charge. But the head only knows logic, what 'makes sense,' and what it has already experienced, which closes it off from conceiving of new and better things. But with the emotions, you don't have to even come up with how it all needs to happen – you just need to trust that you will always have that emotional signal to rely on.

The way you trust this mechanism is not to have blind faith. It's not to meditate on it. It's by trying out this new way of doing things and building up enough evidence that it works, over time, so that eventually, it becomes your new automatic process.

Sacral Authority

Gut Intuition

The Gut is about desire – it knows when it wants something, and it knows when it doesn't. It's not based in logic and can't be explained.

When Life sends you something it wants you to do, you will feel a rush of excitement through your whole body – this is your cue to say yes to it and pursue it. These visceral, physical pulls you feel toward things are the Universe's way of showing you that those things are the right decision.

The Gut is black and white. It doesn't know 'maybe.' You'll either feel 'Yes, I want it,' if it's right for you; or if you're *not* meant to do it, you can feel anything from strongly repelled to just meh.

If something Lights you up when you first come across it, that's your way of knowing you're meant to be doing it. You will *literally* feel your body respond to something before you've processed it mentally. You might feel your body get revved up, or you may perk up, make involuntary sounds that express interest and excitement, or just feel that feeling of *wanting* that thing.

Trust your wants

Society has told us that it's bad to want things, to desire things. We've been told it's better to go for things that make logical sense rather than go for things just because we *want* them. But for you, the wanting is your sacred sign that will never lead you the wrong way. Learning to trust your physical attraction to something, or your repulsion to it, will eliminate so much confusion and light the path ahead of you with so much clarity and simplicity.

Make decisions easier for yourself

Since the Gut speaks the language of yes and no, black and white, it's so challenging for your Gut to give you answers to big, open-ended questions like, 'What's my Purpose?' or even, 'Where do I want to go for dinner?' Your Gut needs specific options to be put in front of it that it can react to. If it's clear and narrowed down, it's much easier.

So whenever you need to decide something, try asking more specific questions like, 'Does a career in fitness sound good? Yes or no?' or 'Would I prefer sushi or Thai tonight?' You'll be surprised at how instantly you feel excitement over something, or not.

If someone else is asking you an open-ended question, you can always run through the options in your head, asking yourself yes-or-no questions. Or have the people close to you ask the questions differently to ensure smoother communication between you.

What to do when you can't tell what your Gut's saying

If you're ever feeling hesitant or mixed up, it's either because:

1. Your Gut has spoken, but for some other reason, you're not comfortable with that response; this is when your Gut directly opposes your conditioning, and they are at odds. In this situation, you don't have to always act on your Gut, at least not in the beginning, but just acknowledge what the Gut is saying. When you at least make note of what it was saying, in hindsight you'll see that it was right, which will make it easier to eventually follow it. You'll build up a bank of evidence to show you that the Gut knows better than the 'Oh, buts.' It's like you turn the volume up on your Gut and down on your conditioning and fears, bit by bit, so that following your Gut becomes your new default pattern.

or

2. You're overriding what the Gut is telling you by thinking about it in your mind. Sometimes you can't feel your physical wants

> because logic has been drummed into us so strongly that it's the voice we hear the loudest. We've been taught that the mind should be in charge of all our life decisions, but the mind can only conceive of what it already knows. Whereas the body is leading you toward possibilities that you might not even be able to fathom but that are so much more fulfilling and Aligned. Trust that the only way you can create a life of joy is by following your joy on the way there.

In order to make the right decisions, you don't need to know why you gravitate toward certain things and not to others; you just need to experiment with following that more, even when you have no idea how it gets you closer to your dream life.

The more you practice the more you'll see the tangible results in your life and then it becomes easier and easier to follow that Gut over time.

Splenic Authority

Instinctive Intuition

Your intuition shows up as sharp instincts. Instinct is the voice inside you that pops out of nowhere, unprompted, giving you messages and direction on what to do. You have this sixth sense because your spleen is the strongest part of your chart, and that's the part of the body that rules instinct.

Unlike the voice of the mind, your spleen is not rational, and you can't make sense of it – it's intuition in the truest sense of the word.

Call them hits, call them pings – they're complete messages that just get dropped in your lap. They bypass your brain completely and work faster than your conscious mind. These are the way your Soul speaks to you about what's right in any given moment.

We've been taught to make decisions in this world based on what's predictable, knowing all the facts first, needing logic and reasoning, and being able to explain our decision. But the instinct can't be explained – it just says what it needs to say and then it's gone. If you feel something you can't make sense of – it's definitely the voice of the spleen.

But if you've been taught to only trust what you can understand, you shun the voice of instinct, and so your spleen gets quieter and quieter, which makes it more difficult to hear.

Notice your instincts

Your spleen gives you direction in the moment, it gives it to you one time, and then it's gone. Whenever you do get those random intuitive hits that cross your mind, note them down in your mind, on paper, or in your phone. By acknowledging that voice even when it's tiny and quiet, you are exercising it, so then it grows. As you build up a bank of evidence of those intuitive hits and look at them in hindsight, you will start to see how and why they were the right things for you, which will make it easier for you to start trusting them and doing what they are telling you to do.

On the contrary, the mind will continue to churn the same repetitive thoughts and fears over and over. So it 'overpowers' the spleen in many ways, unless you really get clear on what that instinct was saying, and hold tight to it as you make the decision. When you give less time and attention to the voice of your mind and more time and attention to your hits, you will come into your full intuitive power. When properly strengthened, the spleen can give you messages about anything and everything, and you can also ask it any question, and it will give you an answer.

Once you are in a place where you feel you've strengthened your relationship to the spleen, and you can't get a clear answer about something, it's only ever because your rational mind is getting in the way. Whenever you feel confused, try to notice which voices are your mind and which are the ones of your instinct.

Strengthening the splenic voice

You can practice strengthening your splenic voice by consulting it on the little things that you don't place so much importance on. For example, what lane should I turn on or which coffee shop should I go to this morning? Have fun with it. This will send the message that you're open to trusting it, so the spleen will start communicating to you more often and more loudly.

The more of a close relationship you build with your instinctive voice, the more you will feel effortlessly guided through life and feel this deep trust in yourself that you can always 'know' where to go and what to do. No overthinking or looking outside of yourself for the answers. You are a strong Intuitive and life gets so much sweeter, juicier, and easier when you put your instincts in charge.

Don't try to explain or justify your sixth sense to others

Be okay with not being able to explain it to other people. If you ever feel like you need to, then the world will bring you tons of situations where people expect explanation from you. The outside world is shaped by your beliefs.

But when you fully own that you do things because that's what you're called to do, the outside will honor and accept that about you too.

Ego Authority

What You Want, IS Your Intuition

The Ego is all about your wants. When you have an Ego Intuition, it means that the right things to choose in your life are the things you want – not what your Gut or emotions or mind tell you, but the things you look at and say, 'I want that.'

This can be challenging because the world has told us that wanting is bad, that you have to suppress or hide any desires for fame, money, success, and impact because that makes you greedy, shallow, or ill-intentioned.

But the only reason having any of those things is bad is when a person goes about getting them with the wrong consciousness. If you believe that someone else has to lose out in order for you to get what you want, if you believe that having these things makes people worthier, better, or more important than others, if you believe in the zero-sum game, then following your wants will create a negative trail of energy behind you. But if those wants are coming from a pure, Soul-led place, they are good and Aligned.

Your wants are your signposts

You have to trust that your wants are Divine. You've been given Ego Intuition in this lifetime because the Universe wants you to listen to those wants in order to get to your Highest Self. Your wants are your signposts showing you where to go.

You don't have to know where you're ending up; you just have to listen to the things your Soul is pushing you toward. You won't always know where and why your wants are leading you. It could be, for example, that you have a huge love karma, and you're driven by money so that you buy the huge house and end up moving in next to your soul mate. So the message here is don't question your wants, they are Divine.

How to hear your Ego

The first and most important step of unlocking that inner guidance from your Ego is getting rid of any judgments and fears you have over your material wants and about what those wants mean about you.

It's all about the consciousness behind your wants

There's nothing innately wrong with money, fame, success, or impact (you'll have your own combination of these that you're drawn to) – if you remove the beliefs we have around these things, they themselves are completely energetically neutral. And the Universe is using them as a carrot to help show you what choices to make and which directions to go in life.

But through the vast majority of history, people have gone about them with the wrong consciousness – either taking from or trampling over others in order to get it or believing that those things would make them better than others. But you can now do it in the good kind of consciousness – honoring your wants and knowing that when you follow them, you participate in creating the best situation for all, even if you don't see how it's gonna unfold yet.

If something promises you money, and you want money, go for it with all your heart. If it's yours, then claiming it doesn't take away from anyone else's experience, it actually ensures the right things get allocated to the right recipients.

Which wants to follow

When the wanting comes from the heart, when you feel on a Soul level that you want that thing and can't even explain why, it's always gonna bring about a beautiful outcome on all fronts. Try to pay attention to the things you want, because you were told they were good to want, versus the things you genuinely feel a heart and soul craving for when you see them. For example, you might have been told that it's good to pursue money, but if you don't have a genuine want for it, focusing on getting it will always feel like an uphill battle. But, if you are meant to be driven by fame, and you follow that over money, you will actually end up with much more abundance than if you were obsessing over making money when it never really grabbed you. All the good and beautiful aspects of the life you're meant to have will come in when you go where your heart grabs you.

Since you've been given these strong wants, you have a duty to go after these things with a good consciousness, to celebrate your materialistic side, and to have it lift more people up rather than suppress, like in the old days.

G Center Authority

Sounding Board Intuition

When you have Sounding Board Intuition, it means that you get clarity on things when you try to put them into words. It's called a Sounding Board Intuition because the answer becomes clear when you express your inner world in the outside world, discussing things and bouncing things off other people. Not because of what those people might say or advise, but because, when you're thinking about things in your mind, they can seem so complex. Whereas when you talk them out, you can hear your thoughts and feelings explained in a much more linear fashion, and it's easier for you to get clarity on how you truly feel about a certain issue.

Watching yourself talk about your thoughts or bounce things off people is crucial for you especially when it comes to big decisions.

Don't ever think that talking things through with too many people is a bad thing. It's not that you don't know how you feel or what to do, it's that hearing yourself voice your full range of thoughts is your process for deciding what to do.

Think about the thoughts in your head like a ball of yarn; they're tangled and hard to follow. But when you express them out loud, you are forced to unwind them into a straight, clear piece of string. And in doing so, it will show you how you really think and feel.

Ways to tease it out

Talking it out with someone you feel comfortable with is always the best option, but if that's not available for any reason, you can try speaking it to yourself and recording it, then playing it back to yourself. And you can use journaling, too, though it helps if you say it out loud ideally because your tone of voice will also give you clues.

The truth is in the tone

Pay attention when you're speaking to the tone in which you're talking about it. For example, you may be discussing an opportunity that your 'mind' has told you is a good idea or that it 'makes sense' or that it's going to get you what you 'want'; but if you sound unenthused when you're describing it to someone, this tone reveals the truth about your real intuition toward those things and tells you it's not such a good idea. The reverse is also true where if you're shying away from something, but you describe it to your friend in a really animated way, then your inner self knows it's right for you but your mind with all its fears and conditioning is trying to override it.

You may have been taught by the world that sitting alone and pondering things is the best way to be self-assured and in control, but for you, getting too contemplative doesn't move your life forward. You'll get there much quicker by discussing them with others, getting clarity from that, and letting your mind be free to think about other things than making your major life decisions. Talking it through is working out your own thoughts, it's not getting other people's advice.

Mental Authority

What 'Just Makes Sense'

With Mental Authority, it makes you by default a rare kind of Projector called a Mental Projector. All the colored centers in your chart are above the Throat, which means that your Mind center, or Ajna, runs the show.

But you have two different sides of your mind: your 'thinking mind,' and your sensing, Intuitive mind – and mastering your Design comes from distinguishing between them and then using each one for the right role.

Thinking mind

A Mental Projector's Purpose is to have a huge, often singular focus in Life: to observe the outside world and develop their specific and unusual perspectives on it. You have the capacity to transcend regular ways of thinking and, thus, to see things in a different, higher way.

Your thinking mind is for this: you fulfill your Life's Purpose when you look around the outside and use it to come up with sharp, useful insights and perspectives that improve the world in the areas you're interested in.

So the thinking mind is the MVP when it comes to the outside world. But it does a terrible job when you put it in charge of you.

Sensing mind

The sensing mind is the part of you that doesn't observe and process: It just knows – and it doesn't quite know how it knows. This is the intuitive part of your mind and the part you're meant to use for your Self, your personal life decisions.

When something is intuitive, you can't explain it or back it up with logic and facts. The sensing mind doesn't consciously 'think' and try to 'figure out' the solutions, it sits back and taps into what it feels makes sense. You could say the first is the 'shoulds' and your preconceived ideas of the right thing, where the latter is tapped into that ineffable Divine Knowing, seeing a layer deeper than 'facts.'

Your job is to just do what makes sense, even when you can't explain why – especially when you can't explain why. In fact, if you can back it up with logic and facts, it's probably coming from your thinking mind and not your sensing mind. When something just feels right to you, regardless of how the outside world feels about it, that's the path to follow.

Lunar Authority

Letting Time Show You the Answers

With Lunar Authority, your Intuition doesn't come from a part inside your body like it does for other Authorities; as a Reflector, your Intuition is coming from outside of you, from the Universe. Pressing for a decision from within is a futile endeavor, and you'll find instead that the right choices are literally dropped into your knowing, crystal clear, in the perfect timing they're supposed to.

You block this because you've been conditioned to find the answer and know right away, which is what can make Reflectors very impulsive and feel like they're always on the back foot.

Since you're a Reflector and can feel like a different person from one moment to the next, the Universe designed that decisions be revealed to you rather than you having to make them based on how you're feeling today or what's going on today.

Since you're only ever embodying one side of all of who you are, any major decision needs to feel right to you in a variety of different moods and feelings you can be in. If it feels good in a few different states and essences, that's when you know it's right.

How much time does it take?

Usually, for bigger things such as love and career, it could take a couple of weeks to a month. For the smaller decisions, wait until you've at least been in two different moods or vibes before deciding. Sometimes, because you can identify so strongly with whichever mood or vibe you're in at the moment, you can become so convinced that that's definitely the right decision. This gives you a false sense of safety and assuredness, which the world tells you is a good way to be. It's in times like this that you have to remember that momentary assuredness and impulsiveness are not the way you come to true clarity. If you make a rushed decision, it might not be Aligned, in which case, any time and efforts you pour into it won't actually lead you where you want to go. So for you, slow clarity actually equals faster manifestation.

You know it's the right opportunity or choice if it still appeals to you, one, two, seven, 10 days after it initially came to you. Your Intuition needs time to really tune in to all the different sides of life and use the whole spectrum to make a choice.

Honor your unique way

Remember, you have the potential for the greatest wisdom available to all human beings – to surrender and let Life show us the way. In order to master this, you have to become totally okay with doing things a little differently than what the world tells you to do. You will only start to trust that waiting it out and trying it on for size works once you see it play out in your own life. So, why not start now?

Chapter 6

Your Profile

Your Profile describes your personality – how you appear to yourself and others.

When you look up your Profile, you'll see it's described as two numbers, such as 3/5 or 6/2.

Each number describes a different component of who you are – the first one describes your inner self, how you are in your own self, and the second describes your outer self, the way you show up to others.

What this means is that the way you see you and the way others see you is always different – and there's nothing wrong or unusual about that. In fact, it's very right. Because you are always gonna be more familiar with your inner world, which others won't see as much. But they will see the way you show up and interact with the outer world.

It serves us to have our own internal world that's not so obvious to others, and an external side of us for the physical world.

There are six numbers in total and 12 different combinations they can be in:

The 1 is the Knowledge Seeker. If your Profile has this number in it, you're here to investigate and learn – doing these is integral to being/becoming your Highest Self.

The 2 is the Natural. This means the skills and gifts you're here to share come so naturally to you that you're probably not even aware of what they are or when you're doing them, at least to begin with. Allowing yourself to do what comes effortlessly to you is a huge part of becoming your Highest Self/fulfilling your greatest potential.

The 3 is the Experimenter. This means that you have to try things out in order to master things – it's no good someone else telling you or reading it in a book. Launching yourself into life is how you fulfill your greatest potential.

The 4 is the People Person. This means you're great at making connections with others, and you have a sense of knowing who and what is right and wrong for you. Listening to that is crucial to your Purpose in this life.

The 5 is the Liberator. It's the person who's great at sorting things out or coming up with the solution for others. They are the people who champion the freedom and happiness of others and everyone having a happy ending.

The 6 is the Role Model. They are great at being and modeling some aspect(s) of what it means to be an excellent human being. You show and give others ways of being to aspire to – not by telling them directly, necessarily, but just cultivating it in yourself so that it radiates out of you.

Let's get into each one and how they come together to form your full personality.

1/3: The Establisher of Knowledge and Truth

1: The Knowledge Seeker

On the inside, you see yourself as an investigator: you seek out facts and information because understanding things, knowing about things, and being armed with the facts is what makes you feel safe. You feel most confident when you feel well prepared. You are someone who finds yourself going down rabbit holes to find information, which may express itself as loving higher education or just Googling everything. The way this expresses itself is unique to you, but just know that this drive to know things is an essential part of you establishing yourself as an authority in this life. The Universe is making you thirsty for information because it's part of your Purpose.

Others may misunderstand this need to know as nosey or a know-it-all, but that's because to them, it would take a lot of inauthentic effort to be that curious. They can't see how it's such a natural draw for you that doesn't require much energy or force at all; to you this is how you develop your genius by exploring and dipping your toes into subjects that fascinate you. Don't judge what the subjects are that draw you to them, they're not always related to the work you do, but they will somehow always help you down the line; even if it's to not just to relay the information but expand understanding, make you more empathetic or give you a transferable skill, there are many ways it could serve you. It's not necessarily about knowledge for knowledge's sake, but that information can be turned into so many other gifts.

3: The Experimenter

On the outside, others see you as an experimenter. Your journey is about testing things out in your life, seeing what works, seeing what doesn't, and getting wisdom from the outcome. The main block to truly embracing this is that our culture believes that when things don't work it's 'bad,' so your natural trial-and-error process can feel like failing. But for an Experimenter, every outcome contains wisdom that helps you get to your next level, if you're willing to see it that way. It's imperative for you to try everything out to see if it passes your standards or not.

You're here to be unafraid to fail, because failure is just a stepping stone to success. The quicker you embrace that some things might not work out, the faster you will get to succeeding. You are naturally designed to live through a trial-and-error process, so find a way to feel powerful as you do it and to see it as fun, interesting, playful. Know that failing at it doesn't make you bad or say anything about you personally, really – it just means that you are unafraid to try things where most are not. You are designed to be brave.

When They Come Together

It might seem counterintuitive to be both a knowledge seeker and an experimenter. The key to blending these two parts of you, is remembering that 'truth' evolves as you evolve. And it will evolve a lot for you, as you have a natural tendency toward being a spiritual seeker. As you move through life and discover new things, you will establish new truths, so don't be afraid to keep moving on from things you previously believed. This is just you going higher and higher in your perspectives and viewpoints. You're someone who is constantly meant to be evolving your definition of the truth. Keep letting go and moving with the changes that Life is nudging you toward.

During this trial-and-error process, you'll seek out other Authorities that help you make sense of it all or of your journey – this is a healthy thing for you to do. You can use them to help you understand your process, but at the same time, you have to feel like you discovered those things for yourself through your own experience. This is very important to you living your Purpose. So it's a balance of gathering intel, but then also testing and trialing it out to see if it passes your test. You're a naturally skeptical person with a healthy dose of questioning, which helps you preserve the fact that you're meant to discover things on your own, but also you can't be lied to as you have a nose for the truth.

Eventually, of course, you're meant to become an authority yourself, but you tend to not like attention until you feel qualified enough. Remember that 'qualified enough' is not a destination – you always have things you'll be qualified enough to speak about, and there will always be more to discover and learn; don't hold off feeling like you have something to contribute before you reach this nonexistent state of 'completely qualified.'

You are the person who knows their s*** – in a way that we can truly trust because you've actually tried it all out and filtered it through your own excellent high standards.

1/4: The Omniscient Teacher

1: The Knowledge Seeker

On the inside you see yourself as an Investigator. You seek out facts and information because understanding things, knowing about things, and being armed with the facts is what makes you feel safe. You feel confident when you feel well prepared. You are someone who finds yourself going down rabbit holes to find information, which may express itself as loving higher education or just Googling everything. The way this expresses itself is unique to you, but just know that this drive to know things is an essential part of you establishing yourself as an authority in this life. The Universe is making you thirsty for information because it's part of your Purpose.

Others may misunderstand this need to know as nosey or a know-it-all, but that's because, to them, it would take a lot of inauthentic effort to be that curious. They can't see how it's such a natural draw for you that doesn't require much energy or force at all; to you this is how you develop your genius by exploring and dipping your toes into subjects that fascinate you. Don't judge what the things are you're drawn to, they're not always related to the work you do, but they will somehow always help you down the line. It's not just about relaying the information but expanding understanding, making you more empathetic or picking up a transferable skill; there are many ways it could serve you. It's not necessarily about knowledge for knowledge's sake, but that information can be turned into so many other gifts.

4: The People Person

On the outside, you're a People Person, which means that the Universe will bring your dreams to you at your door via the people you know. You have a sense of who is right for you to spend time with, and you should listen to that sense: When you cultivate relationships with those who feel bright and Aligned to you, you will be sent bright and Aligned opportunities. Don't be afraid to be a little closed off or disinterested in those that you don't resonate with: it's not that they're bad people, they're just not right for you, and you're not designed to spend time with just anybody. Once you start to honor that and don't judge it as being closed, all the support and opportunities you're designed to have in life will come to you. Who you enjoy hanging around is who you're meant to be around, it's not by accident – so don't question why you're drawn to some and not to others. A huge milestone in your life comes when you really feel like you've found your people. And since you already know the social situations you're meant for, don't judge yourself for being inflexible when a social situation doesn't appeal to you.

For you, the saying is really true: the quality of your life is determined by the quality of your relationships.

When They Come Together

You are here to learn about things that fascinate you and then express those findings with the people connected to you, trusting that everything you want will be brought to you from there. You are a strong, powerful person who radiates authority, and we love to learn from you. When you get this knowledge out by listening to your Strategy, you will attract people who are ready for what you have to share. You're here to establish foundations both for yourself and the people in your life, making us feel more safe and knowledgeable about the world. And you're here to share information about the subjects that fascinate you personally.

In becoming that authority, you find your insecurities start to disappear. Remember that, since you're a People Person, it's easier to become an authority once you've consciously curated everyone in your life.

Know that you are designed to share and educate about things without necessarily going through those things yourself. Once you have learned something and made sense of it, you are qualified to pass it on. The more you do of this, and the quicker you do this, just sharing your findings, the more successful you will be. Feel free to seek out other authoritative figures to teach you, finding mentors you're drawn to will only speed up your process of learning.

It's very important for 1/4s not to engage in niceties, because they will drain you too much. As much as you're good with people, you like to do your own investigating and learning by yourself, you are designed that way, and to have solo creative time.

As a child, you were likely very trusting, so if you ever were told something that wasn't a fact, you may have taken that to be literal because people are so important to you. But remember that mentally organizing information does not come as easy to others as it does for you. In your adulthood, you have to go through your own filtration process where you decide what still feels true for you and what doesn't anymore.

You are here to be a filter and spreader for the highest quality information and knowledge. Trust that what you feel is good info *is* good info, and you don't need anything else to prove it but your own internal standards. We need you, collector of wisdom.

2/4: The Easy Breezy Genius

2: The Natural

On the inside, you're a Natural, which means there are certain things you seem to be effortlessly good at without really knowing how you came to be good at those things or being able to describe to other people how you do it.

There's a pressure in this world to validate or explain how you are qualified to do those things – don't bend to that pressure: in fact, the more people like you are honest about it coming easy to you, the more we'll all realize we don't need to 'earn' things as much as our society has told us.

Coming into your genius is not about learning from the outside world – it's already in you without you really knowing how it got there. When you're doing these things that come easy to you, you slip into this zone where your gifts just seem to come out of you. There is an unaware quality in doing what you do, almost as if it happens without you consciously making it happen. In this way, doing your gifts is quite an unconscious process and takes care of itself as long as you've created the time and space where getting in the zone is possible. But, since it's an unaware process, it's usually easier for others to spot your genius than it is for you, so Naturals tend to require feedback from the outside world to figure out what they're good at.

When you're in your zone, doing your thing, you don't like to be disturbed or interrupted, because you need to be fully devoting yourself to your craft without being thrown off track. So you do have a little bit of a hermit side to you, as it's only through that that you can develop your gifts to the fullest.

When you do find yourself feeling disturbed, you can reframe it by remembering that people aren't usually trying to disturb you on purpose, and also communicating clearly to them when you want to be in solo mode.

4: The People Person

On the outside, people see you as a People Person. Being a People Person means that the Universe will bring your dreams to your door via the people you've made connections with in your life. You are gifted at bonding with people for this reason. You have a sense of who is right for you to spend time with, and you should listen to that sense: the more Aligned your relationships are with your real Essence, the more Aligned the opportunities will be that come to you, whether directly or indirectly. The people you love, you really love, and the rest you can easily go without.

Don't be afraid to be a little closed off or disinterested in those that you don't resonate with. It's not that they're bad people, they're just not right for you, and you're not designed to spend time with just anybody. Once you start to honor that and don't judge it as being closed, all the support and opportunities you're designed to have in life will come to you. Who you enjoy hanging around is who you're meant to be around, it's not by accident – so don't question why you're drawn to some and not to others. A huge milestone in your life comes when you really feel like you've found your people. And since you already know the social situations you're meant for, don't judge yourself for being inflexible when a social situation doesn't appeal to you.

For you, the saying is really true: the quality of your life is determined by the quality of your relationships.

When They Come Together

There's a dichotomy between the Natural and the People Person, since the Natural has a hermit side to it, and the People Person is naturally friendly, and people are drawn to you. The 4 gives you a motivation when it comes time to share your gifts, but the 2 in you also doesn't care that much about sharing. The world will tell you that you can't be both, that one is the real you or that one is better than the other, but both of these sides are here to serve you at different times and for different purposes. Learn to dance between the two, being whichever one the moment needs from you.

Even though you start off unaware of your gifts, the journey of your life is to fully trust and rely on them. Too much studying and filling your head with information will drain you rather than energize you, because that's life's way of telling you that's not really what you're meant to do. You hate being asked what you're up to or what you're doing most of the time because you can't explain it. But others can sense your natural gift, and this will cause them to call on you to share it.

Your physical body can exhaust easily, so make sure you don't say yes too often or you'll get drained and want to shut yourself off from the world even more. You need to have enough recharge time so you have the energy to really GIVE when you need to. It's a healthy balance between being in a secure environment by yourself and answering the right calls to share your gifts, which will draw you out into the world.

You have a natural shyness to you that protects you. This ensures someone's call is strong enough that they actually DO want you to share your gifts and filters out the casual requests. Because you won't just say yes to anyone.

In intimate relationships, your dichotomy also presents itself where sometimes you want to be all over the other person, and other times you just want to be left alone. Be aware also that 2/4s don't see themselves super well, so pay attention to feedback and projections because those will give you helpful clarity that you can't always see yourself.

Your journey here is to have BOTH: your own colorful inside world and a colorful outside world of love, connection, and sharing. And it's only by allowing yourself to have both that you live out your gifts to the full.

2/5: The Reluctant Hero

2: The Natural

On the inside, you're a Natural, which means there are certain things you seem to be effortlessly good at without really knowing how you came to be good at those things or being able to describe to other people how you do it.

There's a pressure in this world to validate or explain how you are qualified to do those things – don't bend to that pressure: in fact, the more people like you are honest about it coming easy to you, the more we'll all realize we don't need to 'earn' things as much as our society has told us.

Coming into your genius is not about learning from the outside world – it's already in you without you really knowing how it got there. When you're doing these things, you slip into this zone where your gifts just seem to come out of you. There is an unaware quality in doing what you do, almost as if it happens without you consciously making it happen. In this way, doing your gifts is quite an unconscious process and takes care of itself as long as you've created the time and space where getting in the zone is possible. However, since it's an unaware process, it's usually easier for others to spot your genius than it is for you, so Naturals tend to require feedback from the outside world to figure out what they're good at.

When you're in your zone, doing your thing, you don't like to be disturbed or interrupted because you need to be fully devoting yourself to your craft without being thrown off track. So you do have a little bit of a hermit side to you, as it's only through that that you can develop your gifts to their fullest.

When you do find yourself feeling disturbed, you can reframe it by remembering that people aren't usually trying to disturb you on purpose and also communicating clearly to them when you want to be in solo mode.

5: The Liberator

You have a 'save the day' energy about you; you love to help people, whether it's strangers or loved ones – you value all people equally. Because of this, and because you're naturally likable, people subconsciously sense that you can help them, guide them, or lead them. Sometimes they might put that expectation on you, whether they know they're doing it or not. Your work as a Liberator is to discern which situations are yours to fix and save and which ones are not. Just because you CAN fix it, doesn't mean you SHOULD fix it. The right things to do are the situations you feel are a good fit for you to apply your gifts to and situations you actually are excited to participate in.

Sometimes Liberators try to fix everything because they want to make everyone happy. But if you step in and fix things for approval and recognition, you'll only deplete yourself and become your Not-Self. When you are doing something that you actually WANT to do, it means it's correct for you. And when you're stepping in and improving the correct situations, they'll actually give you a burst of energy.

In close relationships, it's important for you to feel you're valued for things other than just sorting everything out for people. You may not even know who you are without trying to save people, but only by letting go of this compulsion will you start seeing the other types of exchanges you can have between you and people you love.

When They Come Together

2/5s are world changers because you are here to challenge and alter the status quo. As a 2/5, you love to help others, but you also really like to be left alone. You don't like being around people or in the world so much, but you'll do it when you feel it's really worth it. Unconsciously, you like to be left alone, yet people are always fascinated by you, which is what magnetizes them to you. Ideally, the process of a 2/5 sharing their gifts is to take time away for your talents to build, which will make you totally ready to go when the day needs to be saved.

You naturally come across as a harmonious person, seeming like you have it all together, even though you might not see yourself that way. This can make you subject to many people's projections, even putting you on a pedestal. However, these projections are usually good ones, so use them to your advantage to really help people. When you connect to your altruistic side and lead with the projections that other people make, it will actually help what you're then going to share impact them more deeply. The danger of pedestalization is that it can feed your ego side too much, or it can exaggerate your low self-worth, or you can become dependent upon it to validate any low self-worth. Be aware that you can't actually do anything about people's projections. You may feel pressure to control how you come across, but that will only block people from seeing who you truly are.

As much as you may dream of changing things up in the world, you also have a strong tendency to rebel and retreat if you feel your needs are not respected. This will show up most strongly in intimate relationships, so be aware of what your core needs are and make sure you have explained them to your loved ones. One of those needs is a need for space, so you need to be in a romantic relationship with someone who respects that – and you need to respect that in yourself too. Ultimately, you are here to embrace your love for humanity AND your love of being in your zone, doing your thing, with your attention fully off of what's going on in the outside world.

What you desire most is harmony and peace – and you have gifts that help bring more of that to others too.

3/5: The Great Life Experimenter

3: The Experimenter

Your inside self is an adventurer and experimenter – you like to experience many things, see what works and what doesn't, and get wisdom from the outcome. The main thing that prevents you from truly embracing this is that our culture doesn't see the value of being open to Life teaching us – we feel safer intellectualizing about life rather than really living it. But for an Experimenter, you are meant to trust that Life is the best school possible – and every outcome contains wisdom that helps you get to your next level.

You're here to jump into life with both feet, because you HAVE to taste life and live it to the full. It's a deep need of yours. What doesn't work out is just another stepping stone on the way to success. The quicker you embrace that some things might not work out, the faster you will get to succeeding. You are naturally designed to live through a trial-and-error process, so find a way to feel powerful as you do it and to see it as fun, interesting, playful. Know that failing at it doesn't make you bad or say anything about you personally, really – it just means that you are unafraid to try things where most are not. You are designed to be brave.

5: The Liberator

You have a 'save the day' energy about you; you love to help people, whether it's strangers or loved ones – you value all people equally. Because of this, and because you're naturally likable, people subconsciously sense that you can help them, guide them, or lead them.

Sometimes they might put that expectation on you, whether they know they're doing it or not. Your work as a Liberator is to discern which situations are yours to fix and save and which ones are not. Just because you CAN fix it, doesn't mean you SHOULD fix it. The right things to do are the situations you feel are a good fit for you to apply your gifts to and situations you actually are excited to participate in.

Sometimes Liberators try to fix everything because they want to make everyone happy. But if you step in and fix things for approval and recognition, you'll only deplete yourself and become your Not-Self. When you are doing something that you actually WANT to do, it means it's correct for you. And when you're stepping in and improving the correct situations, they'll actually give you a burst of energy.

In close relationships, it's important for you to feel you're valued for things other than just sorting everything out for people. You may not even know who you are without trying to save people, but only by letting go of this compulsion will you start seeing the other types of exchanges you can have between you and people you love.

When They Come Together

You are constantly dancing with life and here to lift everyone up with the findings of that dance. All the experimenting and experience makes 3/5s the subject matter experts on life, the ups and the downs, the good and the bad, the messiness of it all and the beauty of it all.

The secret to making it work is in the way you frame it. If you can see it all as wisdom and take it all gratefully and lightly – your life will get filled with fun and extraordinary experiences that just keep getting better and better. In this state, everyone will magnetize to you, because even when you're in the uncomfortable, you navigate through it with a lightness of spirit that everybody craves (and life feels so much easier). You can live high highs if you live your Design. It's not to say you won't have challenging moments, but you will know how to alchemize them and turn them into gold.

However, because society praises drama and pain, 3/5s can often feel like they should hold on to the heaviness and hardness of their lows, which only serves to perpetuate the lows. The more we tell the story that it's heavy and hard, the longer we stay there, and it becomes difficult to see that a really, really great thing can come right after a challenging thing.

When you share your life experiences and wisdom with others, with that beautiful lightness of spirit, it makes everyone else feel more unafraid, more excited, and perhaps learning more about the parts that society doesn't always want us to explore. 3/5s are seen as the most relatable and lovable people. This draws people to want to live vicariously through you to learn about your wisdom on life. The world has valued us for what we know, but for you, your value is in what you have learned.

You will feel more harmonious with age, as the experiences you accumulate will have built up more wisdom. People see you as someone who's designed to lead the change and as someone who has something to say, even though you see yourself as just figuring it out as you go. For this reason, a lot of famous people and public figures are 3/5s, because they are the people we want to live vicariously through. Know that with time, as you embrace your life as one big fun, playful experiment, this will build confidence, and you'll feel more comfortable in the value of sharing your experiences.

You don't have to turn your experience into specific guidance and instructions for people on how to live their lives in order to be of service.

service. People will gain so much more just hearing you talk about you personally. Your specialty is experiencing the full spectrum of what life offers, not the nice, neat little theories about life that people like to hear because they sound good. Be careful that you don't edit out the messy parts just to make others more comfortable; it's okay if it ruffles feathers a little, because life isn't always graceful. Since your message is helpful to all kinds of humans, it's good for 3/5s to stay constantly exposed to new people and not to stay attached to people, relationships, and routines. Putting too much energy into forming close bonds will drain you because your life Purpose is to interact with many.

In intimate relationships, you need encouragement from your loved ones the most. Also remember that you're not here to put most of your energy into one person, because you're here to spread your gifts far and wide. You need to be with someone for whom that works just great too.

You are here to see the amazingness of this physical life on Earth the most, you are living it on the front line to report back to the rest of us.

3/6: The Living Contrast

3: The Experimenter

Your inside self is an adventurer and experimenter – you like to experience many things, see what works and what doesn't, and get wisdom from the outcome. The main thing that prevents you from truly embracing this is that our culture doesn't see the value of being open to Life teaching us – we feel safer intellectualizing about life rather than really living it. But for an Experimenter, you are meant to trust that Life is the best school possible – and every outcome contains wisdom that helps you get to your next level.

You're here to jump into life with both feet, because you HAVE to taste life and live it to the full. It's a deep need of yours. What doesn't work out is just another stepping stone on the way to success. The quicker you embrace that some things might not work out, the faster you will get to succeeding. You are naturally designed to live through a trial-and-error process, so find a way to feel powerful as you do it, and to see it as fun, interesting, playful. Know that failing at it doesn't make you bad or say anything about you personally, really – it just means that you are unafraid to try things where most are not. You are designed to be brave.

6: The Wise Sage

On the other hand, you're also born with innate wisdom – you come into this world already wise to Life. For the first 30 years, your connection to your inner wisdom takes a back seat as you try to establish yourself, your goals, and your direction in life. You experiment with putting your energy into lots of different places, people, and opportunities; and this is an important process.

But as you come to the end of your twenties, you usually start to want to be more selective about what you put your energy into because you now know what will reap you the rewards you want and what won't. You start to want to make things feel a little more peaceful and settled for yourself; keeping all the good parts of life that you acquired and getting rid of the rest, which is now just noise to you that pulls you out of yourself. It's usually at this time in your life that you realize,

'Wow, I actually am really wise and intuitive, and I don't need to look outside of myself so much as I used to.'

The path of the Sage is about not getting caught up in the external and coming back to your relationship with yourself and relying on that source of wisdom from within rather than giving your power or validation to others. The journey of the Sage is that others are MEANT to see you as a role model, but you must be the first person to see yourself that way in order for that to happen. You will always feel insecure when you're placing too much focus on what others are doing and thinking; when you feel settled in yourself and tune out the noise, you will reestablish that connection to your natural wisdom. This wisdom is helpful of course for your own life, but it's also imperative for the way you will be guiding, sharing, and showing up for others. As long as you create time and space to hear what you already naturally know, you will always be seen as someone who others look up to for guidance and wisdom.

When They Come Together

3/6s are here to turn chaos into order, experience into wisdom. Even though you are born wise, you are given a crash course in the ups and downs of life in your first 30 years so that you can not only know in your soul, but know in your body what real-life experiences humanity needs help with. Don't ever think this baptism by fire is wrong or crazy or bad, it's actually just part of your education. It was Life's way of reminding you of wisdom that you already knew. Once you've gone through that, though, you are ready to just be the role model figure who already knows their stuff. It's a heightened position where people are kind of meant to look up to you because this draws them to want your wisdom.

Be aware that your seeming perfection may cause others to put you on a pedestal, which can sometimes create distance between you. But, it's not a bad thing for them to see you as a little bit of a role model; don't give in to societal conditioning that says you always have to be relatable to be a good person. Be humble and show your human sides, but also OWN your position of Wise One. This is the magic combination that will magnetize people toward you.

The chaos and the wisdom may seem at odds, but they're actually the same. The chaos gives the real substance to the wisdom. The fact that you will have 'been there, done that,' also earns other people's trust in what you're offering them.

Sometimes, you can feel like half of you wants to live life to the full, and the other half wants to observe life and just chill out. There's no need to choose between the two: you are both. Allow yourself to flow between the two, retreating when you want, and being out in the world when you want. As you get older, that Wise Sage part of you gets stronger and stronger, and you find yourself wanting to create more peace and order in your life. And you become more confident relying on your innate knowings. Your inner contrasts serve a very high purpose, though, because you're here to teach us, ultimately, to embrace our contrasts, which is how we become whole.

Even once you've retreated a bit, you will still feel like the roller coaster finds you from time to time, and you will wonder when does this settle. This only ever happens because life is trying to give you new levels of wisdom, so go into it knowing that it won't last long.

Even though you're here to help us perfect chaos into order, be aware that perfection doesn't become a huge fixation for you personally. Acceptance is a big practice for you. Trust is also one of the most important things to you personally, because it equals safety. In intimate relationships you need to be given a lot of space and tenderness, even though you may always seem like you are fine or have it all handled.

You are here to turn your life experience into things that can help make all of our lives smoother, clearer, and more easy to navigate. Enjoy your own ride, knowing that it's perfectly made to point you right back to the gifts you came to share. You always had them, you just had to remember they were in you all along.

4/6: The Regal Authority Figure

4: The People Person

In your mind, your life is oriented and measured by the people in it. You're gifted at bonding with people for this reason and have a sense of who is right for you to spend time with. For you, the saying is really true: the quality of your life is determined by the quality of your relationships.

It's through the connections you make that the Universe will send you all the opportunities you desire, so the more you create connections that are real and authentic to your Essence, the better fit the opportunities will be that come your way. Don't entertain relationships that don't align with you, as everything that comes through them will only pull OFF your path, rather than closer to it.

Don't be afraid to be a little closed off or disinterested in those that you don't resonate with. The people you love, you REALLY love, and the rest you can easily go without. It's not that they're bad people, they're just not right for you, and you're not designed to spend time with just anybody. Once you start to honor that and don't judge it as being closed, all the support and opportunities you're designed to have in life will come to you. Who you enjoy hanging around is who you're meant to be around, it's not by accident – so don't question why you're drawn to some and not to others. A huge milestone in your life comes when you really feel like you've found your people. And since you already know the social situations you're meant for, don't judge yourself for being inflexible when a social situation doesn't appeal to you.

6: The Wise Sage

As a Sage, you're born with innate wisdom – you come into this world already wise to Life. But for your first 30 years, your connection to your inner wisdom takes a back seat as you try to establish yourself, your goals, and your direction in life. You experiment with putting your energy into lots of different places, people, and opportunities; and this is an important process.

But as you come to the end of your twenties, you usually want to be more selective about what you put your energy into because you know what will reap you the rewards you want and what won't. You start to want to make things feel a little more peaceful and settled for yourself; keeping all the good parts of life that you acquired and getting rid of the rest, which is now just noise to you that pulls you out of yourself. It's usually at this time in your life that you realize, 'Wow, I actually am really wise and intuitive, and I don't need to look outside of myself so much as I used to.'

The path of the Sage is about not getting caught up in the external and coming back to your relationship with yourself and relying on that source of wisdom from within rather than give your power or validation to others. The journey of the Sage is that others are MEANT to see you as a role model, but you must be the first person to see yourself that way in order for that to happen. You will always feel insecure when you're placing too much focus on what others are doing and thinking; when you feel settled in yourself and tune out the noise, you will reestablish that connection to your natural wisdom. This wisdom is helpful of course for your own life, but it's also imperative for the way you will be guiding, sharing, and showing up for others. As long as you create time and space to hear what you already naturally know, you will always be seen as someone who others look up to for guidance and wisdom.

When They Come Together

In your tribe of people, you are usually the central figure influencing, directing, and organizing everybody else. You are often holding court without even trying, and you may find that social situations revolve around you. In this way, you foster togetherness, which is a super important value to you.

Family and friends are everything to you. When you are doing it with the right consciousness, being the king or queen of your circle is a good thing, as it allows you to spread what you came here to spread, which is your warmth, magnanimity, and wisdom.

The world has told you that you have to do things with your head, but your big strength is your huge heart, and directing people with your heart is very different to controlling them with your head. In fact, your main job in life is to open up the heart because that's where 'your' wisdom comes from. This can be tricky for you, because you're so good at controlling things using your head. And opening the heart is scary to you, because you love people so much that you are terrified of rejection. It's only when you actually show this big heart and vulnerability that people will love you even more for it. But when you're disconnected from your heart or pretend you don't have it, you may find yourself judging, pushing away, ignoring, or rejecting others before they can reject you.

One of the main lessons you're here to learn is that you don't need to have such a tight grip on things for situations to work out well and in your favor. As much as you are this director figure, you need to equally learn that you can trust and rely on others as well – and you'll never be able to see what others can do for you if you're always the one insisting on doing everything. For, as long as you insist on doing everything, this will only confirm your fears that you can't fully trust or rely on other people.

This tight grip can cause mental exhaustion and anxiety; the only way out of this is to quit masterminding everything and just let life happen. The only way you can really trust Life is to try letting go and see that it supports you anyway. The more evidence you build up of Life sorting itself out, the more you will trust. And then you'll be free to just be that Regal Authority Figure from a place of joy and sharing your gifts rather than any misplaced fears or need for control. 4/6s often try to control people because they don't trust that everything will work out okay if they don't.

Even though you are born wise, the first 30 years of your life is still full of ups and downs, mostly to do with people. Those relationships are your lessons in life. The main thing you have to make sure you don't do is let those experiences close down your heart for fear of failure and being hurt.

Once you hit your Saturn Return, at around age 28–30, if you've gleaned wisdom from your experiences, your life will begin to settle down a little. Look back on those experiences with appreciation and thanks, and that will help keep your heart open. Be aware that just because you're right about most things, it doesn't mean that you're right about everything. It's okay to look to others for guidance sometimes too. Your regal air is natural to you, there is nothing you have to do to get it, so relax into it. You don't need to over perform, seek attention, or hide from attention.

You are here to balance the wisdom of your head with the wisdom of your heart. And when you do, you crack us open in hearts and minds in whatever you do.

4/1: The Bonus Life

4: The People Person

In your mind, your life is oriented and measured by the people in it. You're gifted at bonding with people for this reason and have a sense of who is right for you to spend time with. For you, the saying is really true: the quality of your life is determined by the quality of your relationships.

It's through the connections you make that the Universe will send you all the opportunities you desire, so the more you create connections that are real and authentic to your Essence, the better fit the opportunities will be that come your way. Don't entertain relationships that don't align with you, as everything that comes through them will only pull OFF your path rather than closer to it.

Don't be afraid to be a little closed off or disinterested in those that you don't resonate with. The people you love, you REALLY love, and the rest you can easily go without. It's not that they're bad people, they're just not right for you, and you're not designed to spend time with just anybody. Once you start to honor that and don't judge it as being closed, all the support and opportunities you're designed to have in life will come to you. Who you enjoy hanging around is who you're meant to be around, it's not by accident – so don't question why you're drawn to some and not to others. A huge milestone in your life comes when you really feel like you've found your people. And since you already know the social situations you're meant for, don't judge yourself for being inflexible when a social situation doesn't appeal to you.

1: The Knowledge Seeker

You are fascinated by life and people. People with this personality tend to love human behavior, psychology, and anything to do with mapping how humans work – anything from the superficial to the deep. You are here to get obsessed with your subject, whatever that subject is, and it's actually a good thing to let it take over your life. Your Soul is going to keep pushing you to grasp for more truth and understanding because you are here to cultivate a huge knowledge base and then get that out to people.

You seek out facts and information because understanding things, knowing about things, and being armed with the facts is what makes you feel safe. You feel confident when you feel well prepared. You are someone who finds yourself going down rabbit holes to find information, so this may express itself as loving higher education or just Googling everything. The way this expresses itself is unique to you, but just know that this drive to know things is an essential part of you establishing yourself as an authority in this life. The Universe is making you thirsty for information because it's part of your Purpose.

Others may misunderstand this need to know as nosey or a know-it-all, but that's because to them, it would take a lot of inauthentic effort to be that curious. They can't see how it's such a natural draw for you that doesn't require much energy or force at all; to you this is how you develop your genius by exploring and dipping your toes into subjects that fascinate you. Don't judge what the subjects are that draw you to them, they're not always related to the work you do, but they will somehow always help you down the line; even if it's not just to relay the information but expand understanding, make you more empathetic, or give you a transferable skill, there are many ways it could serve you. It's not necessarily about knowledge for knowledge's sake, but that information can be turned into so many other gifts.

When They Come Together

You come into this world very light spirited, without any burdens or heaviness. If you do have any heaviness, know that this is from the outside world conditioning you to make you feel like you had to be that way to fit in or be a good, responsible, smart, successful human. You came here to actually teach us that it's the reverse. We're meant to move through life in a light way, and you have to preserve your Lightness at all costs so that you can model it to others.

This Lightness will bleed out through whatever special fascinations and subjects you're sharing with people. As a 4/1, you don't have to look for people to get that out to; you just have to let yourself get obsessed. Get really clear on what your passions are and hone in on them, almost to the point where you have to put blinders on and not let so many external influences and noises take up your time and energy. The people that want to hear your knowledge will find you, or Life will put them in your path. The real work of a 4/1 is closing off from needing to know everything and just knowing more about what truly fascinates you.

You have a very organized mind that can sort complex subjects and issues into very clear understanding in your head. You see polarity, a.k.a. right and wrong, good and bad, and that's actually good for you. Hold strong to that way of seeing things but just know that others don't see things that way, they are not meant to, but you are. Hold on to that polarity when the world tells you to be more gray – black and white is better for you, but only once you have gone through the internal process of asking what is true or good or not. Be careful not to just accept what the world has told you is good and bad, filter everything through your own standards and your own truth before deciding what to stand for.

Make sure that when you're questioning things and finding out what your stand is on it, you don't just do it with your brain (because that's too much pressure) but also based on your heart and passion. If you do just from an intellectual, heady perspective you will feel fatigued because your brain is prone to mental exhaustion. This is Life's way of making sure you always form your viewpoints from your WHOLE self – including your heart and your feelings.

When you are spreading your strong stance on things, no matter what subject yours is, from the serious to the flimsy, people find it very infectious, and they will gravitate toward you. You are here to learn to not go with the crowd and to stick out a little bit, knowing that doesn't make you better or worse, less or more likable, or any other fears you might have about what that means. You came here to be highly individual. In relationships, you need to be with someone who sees that unyielding Essence and is attracted to that part of you. It's very important that you are with people who see and appreciate how individualized you are.

5/1: The Challenge Solver

5: The Liberator

You have a 'save the day' energy about you; you love to help people, whether it's strangers or loved ones, you value all people equally. Because of this, and because you're naturally outgoing, people subconsciously sense that you can help them, guide them, or lead them. Sometimes they might put that expectation on you, whether they know they're doing it or not. Your work as a Liberator is to discern which situations are yours to fix and save and which ones are not. Just because you CAN fix it, doesn't mean you SHOULD fix it. The right things to do are the situations you feel are a good fit for you to apply your gifts to and situations you actually are excited to participate in.

Sometimes Liberators try to fix everything because they want to make everyone happy. But if you step in and fix things for approval and recognition, you'll only deplete yourself and become your Not-Self. When you are doing something that you actually WANT to do, it means it's correct for you. And when you're stepping in and improving the correct situations, they'll actually give you a burst of energy.

In close relationships, it's important for you to feel you're valued for things other than just sorting everything out for people. You may not even know who you are without trying to save people, but only by letting go of this compulsion will you start seeing the other types of exchanges you can have between you and people you love.

1: The Knowledge Seeker

As an investigator, you seek out facts and information because understanding things, knowing about things, and being armed with the facts is what makes you feel safe. You feel confident when you feel well prepared. You are someone who finds yourself going down rabbit holes to find information, so this may express itself as loving higher education or just Googling everything. The way this expresses itself is unique to you, but just know that this drive to know things is an essential part of you establishing yourself as an authority in this life. The Universe is making you thirsty for information because it's part of your Purpose.

Others may misunderstand this need to know as nosey or a know-it-all, but that's because to them, it would take a lot of inauthentic effort to be that curious. They can't see how it's such a natural draw for you that doesn't require much energy or force at all; to you this is how you develop your genius by exploring and dipping your toes into subjects that fascinate you. Don't judge what the subjects are that draw you to them, they're not always related to the work you do, but they will somehow always help you down the line; even if it's not just to relay the information directly but expand understanding, make you more empathetic, or give you a transferable skill, there are many ways it could serve you. It's not necessarily about knowledge for knowledge's sake, but that information can be turned into so many other gifts.

When They Come Together

5/1s are fixers and problem solvers, always coming up with answers and solutions. Others see the thorough, dependable, and constantly curious person you seem like on the outside, but they don't see the work under the surface. The internal life of a 5/1 is a person who does things differently and dares to go against the grain; both of these are equally valid sides of you, and when added together, it makes you perfectly placed to come up with creative solutions, while also making people feel that they can trust the integrity of that solution.

Because others can subconsciously feel that you can help them, guide them, or lead them, AND because you know you could probably come up with a fix for anything, it can be a lot of pressure. 5/1s feel the force of other people's projections and would hate to fall short of them, disappoint them, or let others down. A big life lesson for you is not to measure your worth based on other people's expectations of you. Doing too much of everything will spread your energy too thin and keep you from doing only what you're meant to be doing so you can be the best at what you're meant to do, which is being an authority in your field(s). You're meant to get to a point where you're an authority and to see yourself that way too.

A big life lesson for you is learning that your value is not just what you do for others. In intimate relationships, if you keep doing for others, believing that's what they appreciate you for, you'll never get the chance to feel like they appreciate you for anything else. Your problem solving is meant to be for your Purpose, not for fixing every person and situation just because you can.

Another theme that you have to explore through your life is responsibility. You don't want to take on too much that it makes you irritable and cynical, but you want to take on enough to feel effective and efficient and connected to your Purpose. Now, if you left it to other people, you'd be responsible and available for everything and anything, so it's actually good to be a little protective of yourself, your time, and your energy. You constantly need new projects and challenges because that's essentially what stimulates your special skills to come out. A 5/1 loves the process and not just the end result, and therefore, they're also hyperaware of other people's process. This makes you wise about how people function. Just because this comes easy to you, know that this is a special skill that not everybody has.

You're built to love to get to the bottom of things, which is great – just watch that it doesn't manifest as an insecurity that the foundations might not ever be strong enough or disappear. Good things can be here to stay without you needing to constantly maintain them. The only way you will know this for sure is if you try to let go a little and see how it does actually work out anyway. The more you try this, the easier it will be to trust it.

In intimate relationships, know that it's not necessarily healthy for you to talk about your weaknesses and your vulnerabilities all the time. Don't try and present weaknesses about yourself in order for people to find you more likable and more relatable – they will naturally see your humanness just by being around you. But let others see the brilliance in you just like you see the brilliance in them. Solving problems really is a superhuman skill, don't feel any shame about it. Others are brilliant in different ways, so you should feel confident in owning it.

You are here to solve things in brilliant, unexpected ways. Don't ever be ashamed of it – we need you.

5/2: The Self-Motivated Hero

5: The Liberator

You have a 'save the day' energy about you; you love to help people, whether it's strangers or loved ones, you value all people equally. Because of this, and because you're naturally outgoing, people subconsciously sense that you can help them, guide them, or lead them. Sometimes they might put that expectation on you, whether they know they're doing it or not. Your work as a Liberator is to discern which situations are yours to fix and save and which ones are not. Just because you CAN fix it, doesn't mean you SHOULD fix it. The right things to do are the situations you feel are a good fit for you to apply your gifts to and situations you actually are excited to participate in.

Sometimes Liberators try to fix everything because they want to make everyone happy. But if you step in and fix things for approval and recognition, you'll only deplete yourself and become your Not-Self. When you are doing something that you actually WANT to do, it means it's correct for you. And when you're stepping in and improving the correct situations, they'll actually give you a burst of energy.

In close relationships, it's important for you to feel you're valued for things other than just sorting everything out for people. You may not even know who you are without trying to save people, but only by letting go of this compulsion will you start seeing the other types of exchanges you can have between you and people you love.

2: The Natural

You come across as a Natural, which means there are certain things you seem to be effortlessly good at without really knowing how you came to be good at those things or being able to describe to other people how you do it.

There's a pressure in this world to validate or explain how you are qualified to do those things – don't bend to that pressure: in fact, the more people like you are honest about it coming easy to you, the more we'll all realize we don't need to 'earn' things as much as our society has told us.

Coming into your genius is not about learning from the outside world – it's already in you without you really knowing how it got there. When you're doing these things you slip into this zone where your gifts just seem to come out of you. There is an unaware quality in doing what you do, almost as if it happens without you consciously making it happen. In this way, doing your gifts is quite an unconscious process and takes care of itself as long as you've created the time and space where getting in the zone is possible. However, since it's an unaware process, it's usually easier for others to spot your genius than it is for you, so Naturals tend to require feedback from the outside world to figure out what they're good at.

When you're in your zone, doing your thing, you don't like to be disturbed or interrupted because you need to be fully devoting yourself to your craft without being thrown off track. So you do have a little bit of a hermit side to you, as it's only through that that you can develop your gifts to the fullest.

When you do find yourself feeling disturbed, you can reframe it by remembering that people aren't usually trying to disturb you on purpose and also communicating clearly to them when you want to be in solo mode.

When They Come Together

You are a brilliant and effortless fixer and solver, here to serve humanity, backed by your big, altruistic heart. You're the one who loves to swoop in and make things better for people, and you seem to do it with so much ease. Making things better is just obvious to you, and that's your gift.

But, while helping others is what you live for, you also seek a lot of alone time. Learning when to do which is the key to creating a healthy and successful life. Because it's so easy for you to help and lift others, it can be hard to believe the fact that there is a real vulnerability to you. You are prone to questioning yourself a lot, and ultimately, this is what you came here to overcome.

Before others discover your genius, you have to discover it yourself and put it out there. It's very important that you don't expect the world to discover you, or you will wait forever, and it will only make you want to detach yourself further from the world. Like your name suggests, no amount of recognition or validation from others will get you going, you came here to believe in yourself and be your own motivator. Remember that the 5 in you is subject to many projections, and if you feel the pressure of too many of them, with no self-recognition in place yet, you will be tempted to just give up or not bother. Don't ever throw in the towel, we need you to keep going because you really are here to be a hero. This will be the thing that both heals you and other people.

The alone time you need is mostly important for your body to stay in good health. So, don't allow your mind to take over your alone time (with overthinking, worrying, and projection) as that will deplete rather than restore you. The alone time is for the body, and getting involved in life is what is the part that soothes your mind and boosts your self-confidence. Getting over your fears of your own image and abilities and your high standard of them is your karma, but no amount of thinking will solve it – you have to demonstrate your own abilities to yourself by just giving it a go. The pressure that you feel from others is actually irrelevant, and this will only trigger you for as long as you have pressure and expectations on yourself. Those triggers are not a bad thing, they are just pointing you to the next place where you can self-examine.

You have strong ideals, and beautiful things can be born out of these ideals. You can use them to create and encourage excellence in the world. As long as you don't overly fantasize about life or others, it's actually GOOD to hold strong to these ideals of how good we can all be. When you believe in it, you make it easy for others to believe in it, too, and half of the work of creating an ideal world is having faith in it.

You have a transpersonal karma, which means you will feel most worthy when you're contributing to others. Know that the recognition you crave will come the more you see your natural talents as being valuable and just start putting them out there, and really owning them. It's not other people's responsibility to tell you you're great, it's yours. But ironically enough, when you value those natural gifts you were given, others pick up on that and will value you for those too. You have a karma of letting go of what other people think, which is difficult because you hold yourself to such a high standard. It's time to value yourself. This will be the most healing thing you do and the key to having everything else you desire come to you.

In close relationships, you may find you seek feedback that people aren't always able to give. But just because they won't always be in a space to give it, it's not necessarily anything that's wrong in your dynamic. You open yourself up more for feedback when you show your vulnerability and softness rather than talking about your performance like a science project. People respond best to that big, soft heart. Also in relationships, remember that changing and fixing things is easy and obvious to you; but it isn't to everyone, so don't allow yourself to get frustrated at other people's pace.

The key with being a 5/2 is marrying your effortless brilliance with your huge care for helping humanity. And when you do, that's your gold.

6/2: The Exemplary Human

6: The Wise Sage

The Sage is someone who is born with innate wisdom – you come into this world already wise to Life. But for your first 30 years, your connection to your inner wisdom takes a back seat, as you try to establish yourself, your goals, and your direction in life. You experiment with putting your energy into lots of different places, people, and opportunities; and this is an important process.

But as you come to the end of your twenties, you usually want to be more selective about what you put your energy into because you know what will reap you the rewards you want and what won't. You start to want to make things feel a little more peaceful and settled for yourself; keeping all the good parts of life that you acquired and getting rid of the rest, which is now just noise to you that pulls you out of yourself. It's usually at this time in your life that you realize, 'Wow, I actually am really wise and intuitive, and I don't need to look outside of myself so much as I used to.'

The path of the Sage is about not getting caught up in the external and coming back to your relationship with yourself and relying on that source of wisdom from within rather than giving your power or validation to others. The journey of the Sage is that others are MEANT to see you as a role model, but you must be the first person to see yourself that way in order for that to happen. You will always feel insecure when you're placing too much focus on what others are doing and thinking; when you feel settled in yourself and tune out the noise, you will reestablish that connection to your natural wisdom. This wisdom is helpful of course for your own life, but it's also imperative for the way you will be guiding, sharing, and showing up for others. As long as you create time and space to hear what you already naturally know, you will always be seen as someone who others look up to for guidance and wisdom.

2: The Natural

You come across as a Natural, which means there are certain things you seem to be effortlessly good at without really knowing how you came to be good at those things or being able to describe to other people how you do it.

There's a pressure in this world to validate or explain how you are qualified to do those things – don't bend to that pressure: in fact, the more people like you are honest about it coming easy to you, the more we'll all realize we don't need to 'earn' things as much as our society has told us.

Coming into your genius is not about learning from the outside world – it's already in you without you really knowing how it got there. When you're doing these things you slip into this zone where your gifts just seem to come out of you. There is an unaware quality in doing what you do, almost as if it happens without you consciously making it happen. In this way, doing your gifts is quite an unconscious process and takes care of itself as long as you've created the time and space where getting in the zone is possible. However, since it's an unaware process, it's usually easier for others to spot your genius than it is for you, so Naturals tend to require feedback from the outside world to figure out what they're good at.

When you're in your zone, doing your thing, you don't like to be disturbed or interrupted because you need to be fully devoting yourself to your craft without being thrown off track. So you do have a little bit of a hermit side to you, as it's only through that that you can develop your gifts to the fullest.

When you do find yourself feeling disturbed, you can reframe it by remembering that people aren't usually trying to disturb you on purpose and also communicating clearly to them when you want to be in solo mode.

When They Come Together

The 6/2 is about becoming the kind of adult that your child self would have wished existed: You were born to become your dream human being, instead of needing anyone else to be. As a child, you were already an authority and super wise. You have naturally high standards, big goals, and beautiful ideals. You stand above trivial things and have a gifted ability to just handle things. These all make you the perfect person to be an Exemplary Human.

You like to focus on depth and meaning – and when you own that, you get Aligned. So don't let the trivial and the irrelevant sides of life bog you down; or waste any time judging them. Being a 6/2 is about focusing your energy on seeing how high you can go, don't let it be wasted on where you think others are falling short; this will only bring you into your Not-Self.

Remember this life is about really, fully shining and being extraordinary in yourself. Not compared to anything else around you but compared to your inner ideals.

Because you have very high standards, since you were a child, you probably looked around and thought, 'They could be doing this better.' This life is about actualizing the excellence that your mind dreams of. Because you're so proficient, it can lead you to doing it all and wondering why others can't keep up. This will lead you to feeling frustrated or wondering why you even bother. Resist giving in to these thoughts, because this is the area that you need to learn acceptance. Instead of giving in to frustration, realize that others are gifted in different areas. When you think 'Why bother' or 'what's the point,' – the point is not about other people's reactions, the point is about you meeting your own ideas of self, regardless. Because you are so proficient and such a perfectionist, it's also important to resist feeling superior. The downside of being a perfectionist is that you can also be your worst critic, so, on the one hand you know that you have the potential of being extraordinary, but on the other hand you can question it incessantly. There is also part of you that is resistant to fully allow yourself greatness, even though deep down you know you have it.

The first 30 years of your life can be particularly confusing because of the trial-and-error phase, which can make you question yourself unnecessarily. Remember that those trials and tribulations are only there to give you wisdom, and not because you're flawed. Know that the questioning is simply a nudge from your Soul to keep raising your standards higher and higher, to go above and beyond. Keep in mind that what reassures you is doing things that confirm to you that you are really capable and gifted rather than allowing your mind to think too much about them. It's in the doing and being that you feel good about yourself, not in the thinking and analyzing.

There is a delicate balance between taking on enough that you feel effective, inspired, and powerful, and taking on too much, which is when you'll start to feel like all these responsibilities you signed up for are burdensome. Watch that you don't blame other people for pressuring you or needing you when it was a responsibility that you signed up for in the first place. There is a dichotomy between the 2, which, in you, shows up as unconscious uncertainty, and the 6, which is eternally optimistic. You can tend toward micromanaging, which in itself is not a bad thing, it's just about using it in the right times and in the right ways. You find you can only delegate once you feel that person has shown you that they're trustworthy.

In relationships, it's important you don't focus on where others are falling short and don't make assumptions why they're doing so. You might also try to always improve others – watch that you only do it from a place of love rather than a place of irritation or control.

You are here to become your vision of the best human you can be and, in doing so, show us all how much better we can be too.

6/3: The Responsible Adventurer

6: The Wise Sage

Your inside self is someone who possesses innate wisdom – you come into this world already wise to Life. But for your first 30 years, your connection to your inner wisdom takes a back seat as you try to establish yourself, your goals, and your direction in life. You experiment with putting your energy into lots of different places, people, and opportunities; and this is an important process.

But as you come to the end of your twenties, you usually want to be more selective about what you put your energy into because you know what will reap you the rewards you want and what won't. You start to want to make things feel a little more peaceful and settled for yourself; keeping all the good parts of life that you acquired and getting rid of the rest which is now just noise to you that pulls you out of yourself. It's usually at this time in your life that you realize, 'Wow, I actually am really wise and intuitive, and I don't need to look outside of myself so much as I used to.'

The path of the Sage is about not getting caught up in the external and coming back to your relationship with yourself and relying on that source of wisdom from within rather than giving your power or validation to others. The journey of the Sage is that others are MEANT to see you as a role model, but you must be the first person to see yourself that way in order for that to happen. You will always feel insecure when you're placing too much focus on what others are doing and thinking; when you feel settled in yourself and tune out the noise, you will reestablish that connection to your natural wisdom. This wisdom is helpful of course for your own life, but it's also imperative for the way you will be guiding, sharing, and showing up for others. As long as you create time and space to hear what you already naturally know, you will always be seen as someone who others look up to for guidance and wisdom.

3: The Experimenter

Your outside self is an adventurer and experimenter – you like to experience many things, see what works and what doesn't, and get wisdom from the outcome. The main thing that prevents you from truly embracing this is that our culture doesn't see the value of being open to Life teaching us – we feel safer intellectualizing about life rather than really living it. But for an Experimenter, you are meant to trust that Life is the best school possible – and every outcome contains wisdom that helps you get to your next level.

You're here to jump into life with both feet, because you HAVE to taste life and live it to the full. It's a deep need of yours. What doesn't work out is just another stepping stone on the way to success. The quicker you embrace that some things might not work out, the faster you will get to succeeding. You are naturally designed to live through a trial-and-error process, so find a way to feel powerful as you do it and to see it as fun, interesting, and playful. Know that failing at it doesn't make you bad or say anything about you personally, really – it just means that you are unafraid to try things where most are not. You are designed to be brave.

When They Come Together

As a 6/3, you are super fun AND super wise, being a seeker, but also seeming like you've got it all together. This can seem like a contradiction at times, but your life is about making these two sides come together, you don't have to choose. Responsibility comes easy to you, and you wear it lightly, and at the same time, you want to be free and explore and always experience more.

The key is to remember that experience is just a true form of enjoyment for you. You don't have to justify that there is a purpose for everything. You don't need to give in to the pressure to explain your thinking. You just have to trust that if you're truly drawn to doing something for the enjoyment of it, it's because it will reap rewards for you later, even if you don't yet know what they are. Everything will give you a skill, making your life richer, open your heart more, or help you get closer to your Purpose. If you're drawn to something, own it, and other people will actually respond positively to your actions too.

The mundane is the enemy of the 6/3. You want a full life and that's how you're designed, and you'll bring out that side in others too. When you do come up against the mundane sides of life, be careful not to let that make you feel blue – brush it off and remember that you can always go and create your own idea of fun. Keep your sense of fun and adventure intact no matter how much the world tries to bog you down – we need you to stay high. That's what people actually want from you the most, and also what makes life worth living for you.

Since the first 30 years of your life are extra experimental, it's important not to think you're going through these things because you don't know what you're doing. All that's happening is Life pushing you to live the fullness of life. Don't judge yourself for this: see it all as fun, let it help you feel wonder for life, let it help you see life as being delicious and juicy. You're lucky because, no matter what experiences you go through, that naturally wise side of you has the ability to process it and make sense of it in real time, so, unlike the people who learn the lessons later, you can 'get it' as it's happening.

You have a voice inside you that sometimes tells you – 'This is not it, there has to be more to life than this.' The searcher in you will always tell you there is more. Don't make the searching make you feel inadequate: it's a nudge from your Soul to make sure you keep living life to the full, and for as long as you're alive, there'll always be more. Celebrate that. How wonderful that you have this expansive quality to you that never stops.

And just because there will always be more to experience, it doesn't mean that where you are is not good enough or that you still have to do so much better than you already are. The more you live through things, the more you'll remember that you knew all this deep life wisdom all along and never needed to qualify how you know it.

In relationships, as much as you come across as adventurous, you also really want the safety and trust. You may want to communicate this to your partner as it's always easier for people to see the outside part of you than the inside part of you.

You are here to show us all that we can be wise and always have a huge, playful zest for Life. Don't ever compromise having it all, and in doing so you will lift everyone else up too.

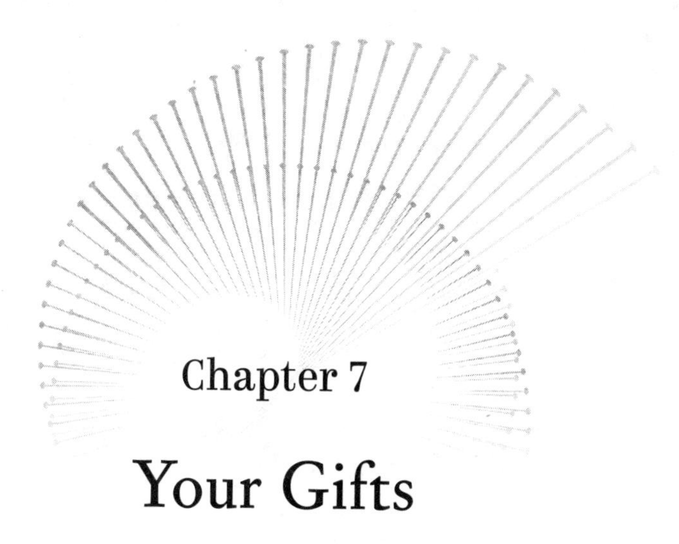

Chapter 7

Your Gifts

You are already equipped with the exact, perfect gifts you'll ever need to accomplish everything you want in this lifetime.

Success is therefore not about trying to 'become good' at stuff or do it the way everyone does it. It's about doubling down on the stuff that you already knew how to do but perhaps never valued or saw as your keys. Success comes to us most easily when we are flexing our innate traits and contributing them to the whole – and allowing everyone to do theirs. It's a perfectly designed system like that.

Your inherent skills and traits are the things the world wants from you, no matter the form they come through you in – being them is your real 'job.' Most of the time, other people don't consciously realize it's what they want, but we all are tuned in enough to sense people who are really in their lane in life, and it's those Aligned people that make us want what they're giving.

How to Find Your Gifts in Your Human Design Chart

If you look at the lines, or 'Gates,' in your chart, you'll see each one has a number that corresponds to it. Each number represents a gift that humans possess.

The numbers you have colored in are gifts that you inherently have. So take a look at your numbers and then read about the corresponding gifts in this section to piece together what your individual magic you bring to the world looks like.

Applying Your Gifts

When we use our gifts, we live our Purpose.

And Purpose is so much bigger than just your work life.

As far as the Universe is concerned, your whole life is a canvas for you to radiate your gifts onto. So your gifts can also help you optimize the way you parent, interact with friends, lovers and strangers, as well as how you create your best success.

When you stop doing your work and relationships the way you think you 'have to' in order to do them right, forcing yourself to approach it the way the outside presents to you as the way, it's like you jump into the downstream, and things just speed up so well for you with less effort. Because you're finally doing life the way you were designed to.

And that's what you came here to do.

Sure, you can make a bunch of money and have four kids without being who you really are, but you have to be who you really are for it to be easier and more fulfilling.

Think about it – trying to be someone that doesn't naturally occur to you requires a lot of effort. And deep down it feels less good.

Two people can have the same kind of house and job and family, but if one is doing it from being whole, and the other is fragmented or doing it from conditioning, the first one will actually be able to enjoy the life they've built so much more – and they'll feel more happy and good on the inside.

How Do You 'See' Your Gifts?

Those small, unglamorous, everyday things you do without even thinking about them? Those are your gifts.

Do you find it easy to get enthusiastic about things?

Do you go down rabbit holes and research things like crazy?

Do you bring people together effortlessly?

Think about your favorite entertainer you just find so sparkly because of their enthusiasm. Or the person in your office with that same gift. Not everyone is meant to have that trait, but you know when you see it on someone, and it just feels right. It's a magnetic power, and one that you have when you get really clear on what your inherent gifts are.

Those are not things that everyone can do, and therefore they are things that other people will want and need from someone else – you.

Know that you can blow any 'small' gift up as big as you like and want, but they will always feel like 'nothing' to you; that's because they're your special thing. When you trust them and share them with others, they will look like pure wonder.

Trust in What Comes Easy to You

All too often, we don't see our gifts as special because they come so easy to us – they're right under our noses, and we assume everyone else is good at them too. We've been taught to believe that it should be a push and a force to make our dreams come true, when it doesn't. Sure, it requires that you apply your focus and put energy into things, but you can do this by using the things the Universe wants you to use.

There Is a Perfect Allocation of Gifts

Of all the gifts available on this Earth, you got the exact ones you needed and none that you didn't. And so did your mother, sister, partner, friend. So we don't need to become anything that we aren't, and if we're all trying to be like another person, it's inefficient for everyone because it's a bad allocation of resources and tasks.

Putting It All Together – The Formula: Gifts + Passions = Perfect Purpose

Your gifts don't tell you what areas of life you're passionate about – your own eyes tell you that (what you're drawn to and interested in, what you could learn and talk about all day).

Your gifts tell you how to apply yourself and what to bring to those areas to be successful at them, because you'll be providing the best possible value you are able to bring. Leading with the things you're good at will always be the best way you could ever possibly be received.

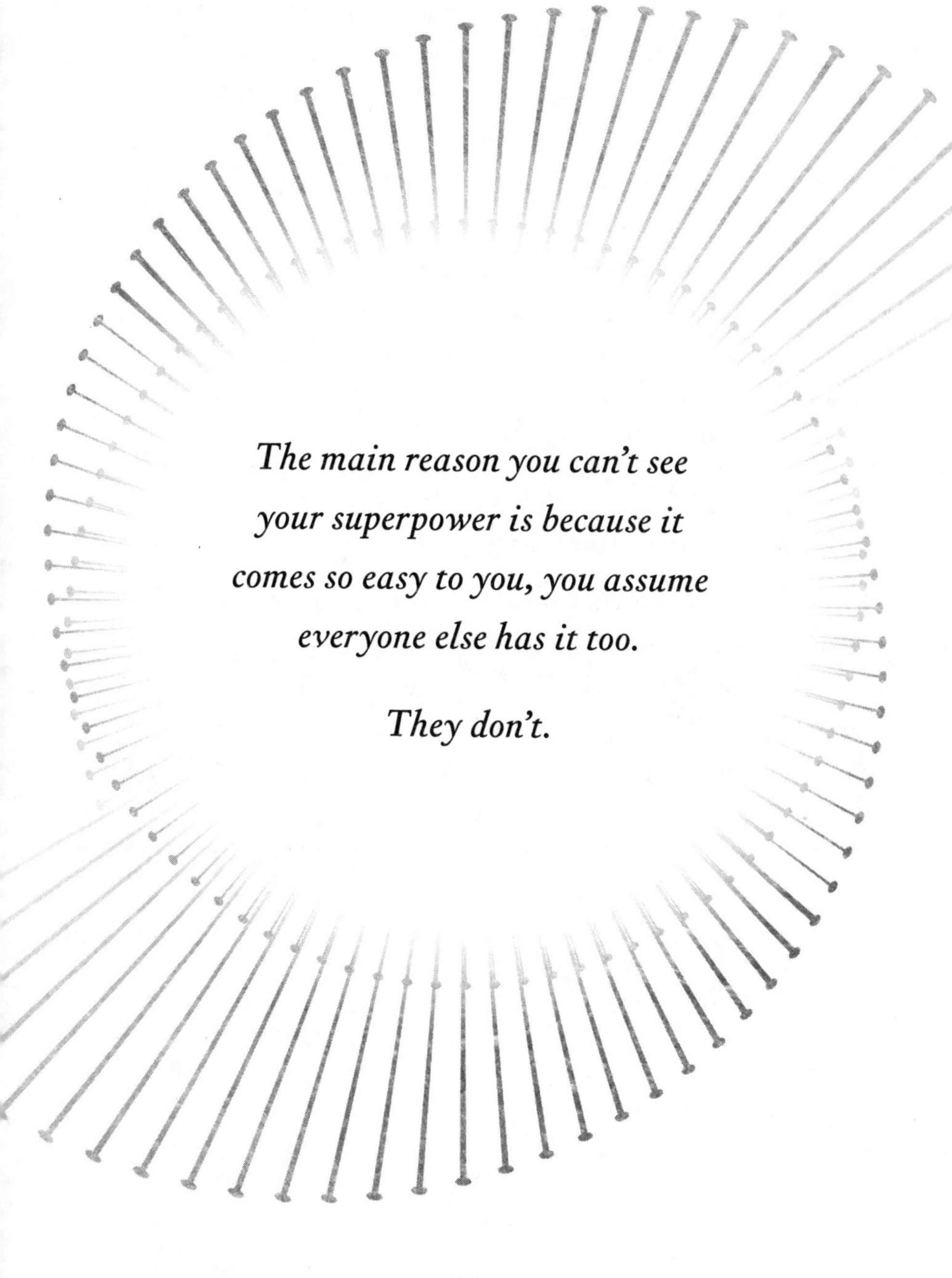

The main reason you can't see your superpower is because it comes so easy to you, you assume everyone else has it too.

They don't.

Let's say you love astrology – if you're good at explaining things, giving one-on-one sessions could be the best use of your time. But if you're a great artist, you might be better off drawing beautiful custom birth charts for people that they can hang on their walls.

If you're a lawyer who has a gift of bringing people together, bring that energy to the way you resolve divorces and disagreements. Or be the one who's helping everyone on your team bond and feel a sense of togetherness, which will also transfer to your work success.

The great thing about living in the time we do is that you can mix your passions and your gifts in any way you can conceive and have it be super successful.

How to Maximize Your Gifts

In today's world, we believe that sharing with a million people is better than one. But it could be that sharing your specific gifts with one person is more Aligned for you, in which case doing that will take you so much farther than just trying to get it out to as many people as possible. It's the quality of sharing not the quantity of sharing – it's the Alignment of your sharing rather than the volume of sharing.

Being loving and kind is not a gift per se; it's the nature of who we all are deep down. It's something you work on within yourself and then bring to any of the gifts you have. The more you share your gifts with heart, the better they will fly.

Gift 1
Newness and Originality

Think of the energy of the number 1: it comes before all other numbers, and it doesn't depend on anything to come before it. This is exactly like you. You're a highly individual, independent person who needs to regularly feel like they're coming up with something new, or contributing to new things, to feel truly alive and happy.

Before anything becomes a reality, it has to be conceived of and created. That's why Gift 1 is the most creative energy in a chart. This creativity doesn't just mean artistic creativity – it's about bringing down new products, services, new ways of doing things, into this Earth.

You are at your happiest when you feel like you have newness and freshness to focus on.

The opposite is also true – whenever life starts to feel repetitive or mundane, you can start to feel like you have the life and joy sucked out of you. For this reason, you can feel prone to melancholy or depression when you're not feeding your thirst for imagining what's next.

How to Flex This Gift

Remember your individuality

Society will constantly convince you that it's better to be how the majority of people are, but for you, it's important to notice the unusual things about you and to emphasize them. This will always make you feel more powerful and capable.

It's also important that you don't ever feel you rely on other people, whether that's for your happiness (because for you, it comes from your connection to your creative genius), for security, or for money. That will always make you feel uninspired and trapped and keep you out of your creative potential.

What keeps many people out of their creativity is a fear of being *so* individual that it would lead to rejection, judgment, or separation from society or their loved ones. But this couldn't be further from the truth, which is that when you share your Light, it's a deep form of loving people. The greatest experiment you will ever take is to be your most individual self and discover it only improves every way you experience. And life will constantly nudge you to go there when, on a Soul level, you'll feel like *not* being individual costs you too much. Fulfilling your job in this life requires that you feel like you're on a forefront in some way, coming up with new, fresh ways and ideas.

How to Unblock This Gift

Make peace with the death and rebirth cycle

Even when you're totally in your creative genius and sharing that with the world, know that creativity (and therefore happiness) will flow to you in a way that you can't always control. Some days you'll wake up and feel super creatively inspired and, thus, full of excitement and joy again, other times you'll feel uninspired and, therefore, a little blue. This is part of life for everyone but is exaggerated in a person with Gift 1. The key is to remember they are part of the cycle of creation: since the 1 is always renewing and regenerating itself, old things have to die or disappear first to make space for the new.

When you *do* have low moments, remember they are not 'who you are,' they're just the weather. They say nothing about who you are as a person, how well you're doing at life. As long as you're engaging rather than sitting on the sidelines of life, trying to avoid it for fear of the low parts, you are on the right path. The more you lean into it, the more fulfilled and alive you will feel, and the more creativity will flow to you. There will always be times you *don't* feel connected to your creativity and bringing new things to another(s). You can use those low points in the creative wave as a nudge to dig even deeper in your endless well within: imagine things you haven't imagined yet about what's possible in life. There's nothing more exciting to you than pushing the bounds out even further.

Don't judge the blue moments as being worse than the pink ones – the blues are a sign telling you when to go inward, to be more mellow, to explore those sentiments – because there is creative gold and aha moments in those too. There is constant dance between Light and Dark, melancholy and happiness – one can't exist without the other.

Surrender to your creativity and its wave

Whenever you feel disconnected from your creativity, retreat and be alone. If you try to look outward and engage in the world to help you escape your uninspired or lifeless feelings, it may temporarily make you feel more stimulated, but remember that you're here to bring in new things, and what's out there in the world is already 'old' to an extent. True inspiration, genius, and aliveness will come from being with yourself.

Whether you're part of a team or self-employed, you need to have ample time working and creating by yourself. The same goes in relationships; you need your alone time because that's what strengthens your connection to Self, with its own thoughts and ideas.

Gift 2
Bringing Things into Form

People with Gift 2 have a talent for being practical, being organized, and able to turn concepts into reality.

Everybody loves being around a 2 because they are great executors. If you come to them with this awesome idea, the 2 knows what you need to do to pull it off, *and* how to make it look good too.

They effortlessly see how concepts and dreams can be brought to life. Sure, it's wonderful to have an idea, but to make it real, you need to give it form – with a structure, with a plan, with a container.

Each person with Gift 2 has a unique way of bringing form to concepts that is totally individual to them.

How to Flex This Gift

Save your gift for your specific niches

The ideal is to provide structure and form, but only when it's part of you sharing your calling or specific genius – don't let it permeate into every area of your life. Let's say you're really good at structuring a deal, and you do that for work. You could apply that to also helping your romantic partner map out a project they're working on – just don't let it also make you believe you need to tell them how to shop for the groceries. But if food and nourishment is your *thing*, then by all means help them buy groceries in a better way – and maybe even do it for others and get paid for it. Conserving this gift and not wasting it on the wrong stuff is the easiest way to get even better at your craft, because you've freed up new reserves of potential.

What Blocks This Gift

Not leaning on others

The negative side of organization and order is control. It's so easy for the 2 to be responsible and directing everyone around them that it can lead to believe that they *always* have to be controlling everything for things to go well. They can get into a situation where they don't think others are capable of doing anything without them, and worse, they don't believe that there are unseen forces at work, much more powerful than any human, that are constantly there to support them. The irony is that the more we feel we need to have a tight grip on life, the more evidence shows up around us to confirm that. There is no space for synchronicities, for things effortlessly sorting themselves out, nothing 'happens' unless you're pushing and forcing it to. So you keep believing it has to be so.

Whereas, when you use your natural gift only when it's actually helping, you Live your Purpose, and not wasting it on the things you're not meant to be directing, you actually will develop the gifts of the 2 so much more, and the other areas of life will just seemingly fall into place.

Even when things feel like they are 'out of order' to you, they are actually perfectly in order – because challenges and problems and rock bottoms are here to catapult us into new learnings and new levels of growth. They are here to push us toward something really, really good. When a problem arises for you, practice asking what good thing it could be pushing you toward. Challenges and problems are something we can transform, sure, but we also don't want to plaster over them so fast that we miss the gift. As for other people's chaos, sometimes the greatest gift we can give them is the ability to be in those situations themselves, without intervening, so they can get the gift that's waiting for them on the other side of that.

Gift 3
Innovation

People with Gift 3 are here to turn chaos into goodness.

There is an aspect of the human experience, or Life, that you came here to transform into something more enjoyable.

In order for Gift 3 people to be able to do this, Life will make them feel *really* inconvenienced or pained by the aspects of life they are here to improve. Whatever affects you deeply is what you'll be most wanting to change, not just for yourself but for everyone. But usually, you'll be moved to want to change it for yourself first. And it's likely that Life will make it something that saddened or maddened you personally so that you are really familiar with the negative experience of it.

If you are ever wanting to get clear on what your contribution in life is, think about what aspects of life really gripe on you. What really frustrates or upsets you. What feels like such a roadblock or stands in your way. Think as far back as you can, because Life can introduce these inconveniences as early on as you can remember.

This gift is about overcoming difficulties in the beginning and using it as a signpost toward something that'll make it nonexistent.

You're here to introduce a new way of doing it, a new solution, new product or service, or way of doing things, a new approach or understanding to it.

How to Flex This Gift

Don't solve the problem from the level it was created

This gift is really tied to innovation and ideals. So it's important you create new alternatives based on your vision of a dream scenario instead of trying to think at the level of the current problem.

Elevate your viewpoint up higher and see it from there. Ask yourself if we were starting from a blank slate, how would we ideally do this?

Staying connected to your idealistic side is important, because it's crucial to having fun for you. Seeing this process of invention and innovation as a playful thing, rather than a burden or a duty, opens your heart, which in turn opens up your energy for you to receive more of those genius innovations. If you don't, things start to feel hard and heavy for you, because, remember, you are programmed to extra-notice the inconveniences and less-than-great ways we're going about things currently. Work on knowing that this is all here to catapult you to your success. If it was all already ideal, we wouldn't even need to come here. And don't shame yourself for those negative reactions you've had along the way, for they held keys to your genius.

A key to being your most innovative self is not staying attached to old convictions or principles that don't fit in with your newly elevated viewpoints. So keep discarding old versions of you – this will keep elevating you higher and higher.

How to Unblock This Gift

Dance with the chaos

We've all been taught to be afraid of chaos, because it means something or someone is 'wrong' or 'bad.' This can hold you back from being in your genius, because ideally, when Gift 3 sees chaos, it looks straight at it because it sees it as an opportunity or portal for invention and innovation. You may not feel overtly 'afraid' of chaos, but notice the times when you even unconsciously ignore it and just keep moving on, or feel powerless over it. Negative things that happen make you far from a victim – they come into your life to GIVE you power and reconnect you with your zone of genius. The Universe actually creates solutions first and uses the 'problem' simply as a gateway to lead us *to* the solutions. So remember, there's nothing bad that will happen to you by connecting to that pain or inconvenience.

Create space between that thing and you, by picturing yourself up here and the problem down there, at your feet, at your service. It was never bigger than you, scarier than you, carrying a damning sentence. It was Light in disguise.

Gift 4
Logical Brilliance

Those with Gift 4 have the gift of an effortlessly brilliant and strong mind.

Logic and analysis comes easy to you – you don't even need to apply any discipline to your mind; it's actually fun for you to look at any subject you're interested in, deconstruct all its various pieces and aspects, and glean intelligent conclusions from this process.

You can look at a complex scenario, separate the meat from the fluff, and see all the important intel it's trying to give us. You can distill things down and spot truths – whether that be around human behavior, financial markets, whatever you enjoy mentally toying with.

What's more, your capacity for analysis and thinking is endless. Your mind is restless in its search for truth. You may assume everybody has this ability because it comes easy to you, but remember that most of the world can't do what you do, and there is true value in your applied mind for the rest of the world. You are here to bring us insight to things we can't see ourselves.

How to Flex This Gift

When it's a subject you're interested in, your mind literally doesn't. tire. out. It's important you realize that an inexhaustible mind is a form of genius, and that it brings you insights and ways of seeing things that others with shorter attentions can't access. Your patience for discovery and willingness to make sense of things is a true gift – and not just to yourself but also to the ways you will use it to contribute in life.

We live in a world that already values logical thinking and reasoning, so it's likely you haven't had much problem spotting and owning this gift – unless you are afraid of being a person with such a sharp mind, because conditioning told you it was bad or unsafe.

Or sometimes, if what you're interested in isn't a subject that we traditionally think of as 'intellectual,' such as interior design, you might not see that you're being unusually logical and insightful in your approach toward it. When you recognize this in yourself, you 'own' that part of you, and it radiates out to others so they are more likely to want and ask you for your genius too.

What Blocks This Gift

Using logic for everything

The key to really strengthening this genius is knowing which situations to use it in and which subjects it doesn't belong in.

Your mind is so brilliant and sharp that it will come up with intricate and airtight logic to support anything you want to be true – no matter what's behind that wanting. If a mind with Gift 4 feels insecure, it can use its brilliant logic to prove or justify these negative feelings about people or things and then present them with conviction and perfect construction that they 'make sense.' But just because something makes sense, it doesn't make it Truth.

Ironically, when you release the need to fit everything into a framework or analyze everything to the nth degree to feel more safe, so much more reveals itself to you. The trick is not to fall back on the mind to reassure you whenever you feel insecure or uncertain, but to use it when a subject really grabs you and fascinates you.

Your challenge is to recognize the difference between your emotions and your logic.

You can tell an emotional reaction when you feel charged rather than neutral and detached about a situation. When emotions are concerned, this is not an area for Gift 4 to apply itself. When you feel triggered or insecure about something, resist the urge to justify these feelings away using your mind. It may make you feel better in the moment, but in the long term it will keep you more attached to these feelings that don't ultimately serve you or feel good. When you justify a negative feeling, you are cementing it as reality, whereas when you detach from it and think of a different way you'd like to see it or feel it, you create a new template for your behavior going forward.

Gift 5
Synchronicitous Timing

Those with Gift 5 have a knack for Divine, perfect timing and living in flow. When they're being their Real Self, they are unfussed about making their day look like everyone else's (e.g. wake up at 7 a.m., at your desk from nine-to-five with a lunch break at 1 p.m.). They are built to time their day unconventionally, and that's for a good reason – because that's the pace that's going to bring out the best in them.

Deep in your bones, you *know* Life isn't meant to be a string of groundhog days that we're enslaved to – it's a much more organic flow. Sticking ourselves into a rigid routine is like putting blinders on – you leave no space for synchronicities and opportunities to pop into your field, much less be able to follow where they take you.

Gift 5 people know we're not here to be stuck in a timing structure and that, when we let go of that, we're much more able to intuitively be and go where we're feeling pulled to at the time we're feeling pulled to it. We miss so much by prestructuring our lives, and for you, Gift 5, that feels especially restrictive. If you've been setting up your days like the rest of the world until now, it's likely been weighing heavy on your spirit and draining your energy.

How to Flex This Gift

Find your preferences

It's time to ask yourself, 'What would feel better to me?' Maybe you're a night owl or you love to get up super early, maybe you like taking naps in the middle of the day. Whatever feels natural to you in terms of timing, that's what you're meant to do. That's the Universe trying to put you in the right places at the right times.

And in doing so, you're here to show others this new and better approach to living life and honoring our innate energy patterns as a way of maximizing your potential and your happiness.

This isn't just about what feels good to you at the cost of 'not keeping up' with the rest of the world – because when you're brave enough to detach from being so 'in' your daily routine, you can see so much more clearly. Your consciousness will start to elevate. You'll spot so many more things you previously couldn't. These are the very things that fast-track you to success.

What Blocks This Gift

Rigidity

If you've been conditioned with fear, a person with Gift 5 can feel the opposite of their Design – like everything is out of order, and that nothing goes well unless we stick to rigid rules. If you feel this, know that it's not 'bad' – you came here to transform this fear in yourself, transform it into something way better, and model it for everyone else.

We often praise people who don't make time for themselves and the little things in their race to the top. But the two things are actually unrelated to each other. Winston Churchill for example, took a nap every afternoon while he was Prime Minister of England during World War II – and still won the battle. If a ritual is calling you, it's for a reason. Don't be afraid to follow it, and you'll see it will give back to you in a myriad of ways. How much value you provide to others is in the quality and intentionality of what you do, not how much you sacrifice yourself for it.

Gift 6

Intimacy

Those with Gift 6 are effortlessly skilled at creating closeness and intimacy with people.

Most of us walk around with barriers up that prevent this bonding. A person with Gift 6 has a natural warmth and strength that breaks through these barriers and makes people feel safe enough to let their guard down. This is the meaning of true intimacy: being comfortable enough to just be who you are, without the need to front or protect. This gift is about breaking down your *own* barriers so that you can get the party started.

How to Flex This Gift

Give yourself permission to bond in a deeper way than 'normal'

Make no mistake: this is one of the most valuable gifts you can have, both for bringing meaning and depth to your relationships and for helping you manifest your dreams. A warm person like you magnetizes people and opportunities to you like crazy when you are unafraid of creating closeness with anyone you might meet. It requires a total acceptance of who you are so that you're transmitting the message of being totally comfortable in your own real Essence – which then sets the tone for all your interactions. *You* are the tone-setter, so make sure you come correct, and it will be one of your greatest assets. You can pierce straight through to people's Real Selves and have them interact with you from your core. This is not something you have to force, it's something that you have to allow. And to allow it, you just need to get out of your own way.

What Blocks This Gift

People pleasing

With this gift, you are very commonly loved by others. The negative expression of this gift is becoming so used to being liked as a source of validation or worth that you become a people pleaser. This, in turn, limits Gift 6, because, if you're interacting with the aim of being liked, it blocks your organic bonding ability.

Pushing people away

But being truly close to others can leave us feeling exposed, at risk of judgment, or hurt. Sometimes it's easier to be intermittently distant or cold as a form of protection. A big potential for healing in your life is when you decide that sure, it's scary, but it's worth it for the potential of deep love and closeness.

Being unnecessarily confrontational

This ability to break through people's barriers also gives a real force to your presence. Another potential misuse of this gift is applying too much force, being confrontational, or frictionous with others, because it makes you feel your own power and strength. This is not real power. Use your ability to touch people deep in their Souls to leave something good behind, wherever you go.

Gift 7
Integrity and Virtue

People with this gift are here to be role models for behaving with integrity in everything they do. There is a pureness to their Soul, because doing the right thing is so important to them. Choosing between what might benefit them versus doing what they know is the right thing is a no-brainer for them: they will always do what's right.

In this life, you came to behave in an exemplary way. This makes you a leader because others see how highly you conduct yourself and then see you as someone who can show them how to be better themselves. You may have never chosen to be a leader or want to be a leader in the traditional sense of the word. But when you're embracing this gift, others see you as a virtuous example which they can aspire to or use as a north star to help them show up in the world.

How to Flex This Gift

No matter how much integrity you already have, know that there are even higher heights available to you; look for the little ways you could become even more of an upstanding, excellent human being. One that you would be in respect and admiration of. Ask yourself, 'What would the exemplary version of me do here?' And then go do that. Rinse and repeat.

As soon as you've conceived of how to do better, you've unlocked the codes in you to be able to be that.

What Blocks This Gift

Conditioned judgments about being virtuous

We've been taught that naturally virtuous people are better than those who have to learn it. In a person with Gift 7, this can manifest in two ways.

1. Being afraid of being that shining example because being better than others means:
   - the fear that people will look at us and think, 'Who does he think he is?'
   - the fear that it would distance them from other people or stand out too much from the crowd, which we then equate with receiving less love
   - the idea that being our most wonderful self is 'bad'
2. Letting your easy virtue make you feel superior to others. For others, virtue doesn't come as easy, and it's a gift you got given so you could help others get there too. There are other things that come easy to them that don't for you – we are all here to share from our easy.

Gift 8

Tastemaker and Marketeer

Those with Gift 8 have an eye for style and beauty. They are people who can just spot what looks good and are here to help us see them, too, for our own benefit and pleasure.

Gift 8 people will present things they like in their most attractive way to others. Whether you create them yourself or not doesn't matter to this gift; it just wants to be the tastemaker. Anything that is created on this planet, whether a product or service, piece of art or clothing, needs a tastemaker who will bring it to the attention of a person who might be interested in it. This is where you shine because you are able to sift through the sea of beautiful things and present it to people who might want it.

How to Flex This Gift

Unapologetically create your version of a beautiful life

Like all gifts, this ability to bring more beauty into people's lives is the value you add to all areas of your life: with your work, with your loved ones, and in the everyday moments of life. Putting time into the way you look and dress, for example, is not a superficial use of your time then; it allows you to flex your gift and advertises your energy correctly to other people.

Don't have any shame over your love of making things look good to others; it's not 'fake' or 'inauthentic' when it comes from a true passion and love, like it does for you. People don't always know what they like and need help spotting and recognizing it through your eyes.

At the higher expression, this gift is connected to its own individual taste, without the need to conform, and without the need to explain its taste. The more you own your individual taste, the more you activate the influential energy of this gift, which then means more people gravitate toward you to receive your guidance on style and beauty.

What Blocks This Gift

Following conditioned norms of aesthetics

At a low expression of itself, this gift is overly concerned with fitting in and following along with what the conventionally agreed standards of beauty are. This can lead them to living very surface-level lives, where their focus is on the superficial and artificial. Beauty itself is not superficial, it's one of the main reasons we came here (to have and experience beautiful things), but when a person with Gift 8 is overly concerned with societal norms, their taste is dictated by the outside world, which removes the depth of this gift.

Gift 8 people have strong discernment, and so sometimes this discernment can lead them to be too dismissive or judgmental of those who don't value taste and style to the same level that they do; remember, if everyone had the gifts you do, you wouldn't have as much value to bring to this world, so it's actually a good thing that they don't.

Gift 9
Momentum Creators

People with Gift 9 find it easy to focus and dedicate themselves to making a dream happen – and they pay attention to even the tiniest elements that contribute to getting them there.

A small act done once won't lead anywhere, but Gift 9 knows that once you've done something once, you've created a template for it, and it becomes instantly easier to do it again tomorrow. Eventually, after the repetition of it so many times, it barely requires any energy from you, yet it creates momentum; things accumulate in exponential manners. You have the power to automate so much in your life that you barely feel like things are a push or a force at all.

The law of momentum is that the more you do something, the easier it becomes to do, and the less energy it then requires from you. Therefore, Gift 9 is a person who really loves efficiency, because success is actually the result of you getting to your most energy-efficient state.

If this is you, you may be thinking, 'Well, doesn't everyone?' And the answer is no. Not everyone understands this principle so deeply. You are here to master it and, in turn, facilitate it for others too.

Remember that even the smallest changes in daily thoughts, intentions, and actions can redirect the ship in huge ways – a one-degree turn today can change the destination entirely. And since you have the ability to see these tiny details, use them. Comb through all the little things that are a part of you and the way you move through your day.

Since our gifts apply to all areas of our lives, Gift 9 people are also gifted at seeing the little things others need to implement or change to get them where they want to go – whether that's with career, love, health goals, etc. The areas you'll be able to do this in are the areas you yourself are passionate about.

What makes that first step so powerful is intention. And once you get clear on your intention behind it, Gift 9 barely requires any discipline for you to keep doing it. You build natural momentum.

How to Flex This Gift

Direct your focus to things you actually like

Just because you *can* apply and dedicate yourself to something, it doesn't mean you should. The world praises us for just working hard on anything, period – but for your efforts to actually lead somewhere good, you have to make sure it's something that resonates with you beyond a surface level.

You've probably put time and energy into really getting something off the ground before, only to realize that that thing doesn't really fulfill you. Then, you have to waste even more energy trying to unwind or get out of it. This is not Gift 9's idea of a good time. Save yourself the time and heartache later by taking time to direct your energies properly when you're starting.

What Blocks This Gift

We know that the first step is the hardest. But Gift 9 people also want it to be easy (since they love efficiency and hate wasting energy).

So sometimes, they can be so turned off by the relative inefficiency of the first step that it can lead to avoidance of getting things moving and started, which manifests as lethargy or lack of passion in a person with Gift 9. Energy begets energy, but the opposite is also true; the longer you don't start, the harder it becomes.

Keep reminding yourself that it is always hardest at the beginning of a project, endeavor, or new habit. BUT: the level of effort required to start the journey doesn't continue to be that way!

Worrying so much about how to make success happen gets you too much in your mind, where the key for you is to focus on your physical habits and actions and not think about it too much. No matter the rest of your Design, you have the staying power to stay devoted to your goal.

Gift 10
Being in Love with Life

Gift 10 wants to fall in love with life, to feel wonder and amazement toward it more than anything – and it's also what they're here to spread.

Gift 10 knows loving life is something you practice doing in every moment not something that gets dropped into some special people's laps when they've achieved *x*, *y*, and *z*. And you practice doing it by having the awareness of just how unlikely and divined and incredible it is that you are here, alive, right now.

The lesson of Gift 10 is that this wonder and amazement is *always* available. When Gift 10 is at its best, it can be at the airport in a five-hour delay, for example, or going through a break up, and lean into the living and being in it rather than live in the negative stories the mind wants to tell about it.

How to Flex This Gift

A person with Gift 10 is someone who feels alive and Lit up by life. And by doing so, they will make others feel more alive too.

Gift 10 connects us to how unfathomably incredible having a human life really is; and they transmit this feeling whenever they're feeling it themselves – it won't require teaching or telling people about it necessarily. It's a much more subtle energy than that. You can be a florist and make people feel that way through your beautiful bouquets, or you can be a dentist's assistant. It doesn't matter. This is a contagious energy that spreads without you even intending for it to.

Try to soak in life as it's happening, instead of thinking there's still something else that you're not doing yet, that you need to do, and that will create a happy life.

How to Unblock This Gift

The trick with Gift 10 is remembering that loving life comes from feeling so lucky to be alive, going through what you're going through today, rather than this giant quest to get somewhere you've told yourself you're so far away from.

When a person with Gift 10 is on their quest to fall in love with life but doesn't quite feel it yet, their tendency will be to look at themselves and think they're doing something wrong that's keeping this happiness away from them. They think: 'When I change this, I'll be more happy.'

But for as long as love of life is based on life looking a certain way, it's not a true reverence and respect for just being alive itself.

Since they want this so bad, they will usually explore any and every avenue(s) they believe will help them. They can end up obsessing over spiritual work or personal growth in a negative way, where it's affirming how far they 'still have to go' in order to be happy.

They could also end up obsessing over their identity, keeping their identity, needing to know and label 'who they are,' or be scared that others may take away that identity or their freedom.

Although these seem different, they are really two sides of the same coin, which is self-obsessing to get to happiness.

Remember: many people who already have what you desire *still* don't feel so alive and Lit up by life. It's our natural state of being, but we give it up when we get raised to prioritize other things. You are here to make the journey back to it and to help everyone else do the same.

Gift 11
An Ideas Person

Gift 11 is a person who is constantly being flooded with new ideas – whether that be for products, services, or creations. You are given this gift to be a receiver of concepts and ideas from Source, not just for yourself but for others too.

You can make a career out of this alone because the world is so in need of new, better products and services that will help create a more beautiful, happy, well-functioning world.

These ideas don't come into your head as words – they come in as abstract flashes of insight or images. This is because ideas originate from the unseen world until someone like you picks them up or channels them into the world of the mind. You may not even realize this, because you're able to translate them into fully formed concepts so easily. But know that your skill of translating energy into form is at work here.

You may assume that having ideas is the fun or easy part, and doesn't everyone have them? And the answer is no; some people, for example, are amazing executors who are just dying for a damn good idea to turn into reality.

How to Flex This Gift

Clear your mind

The more clear and empty your mind is, the more available it becomes to download a constant stream of concepts. The practice of un-busying your mind, removing distractions and negative thought loops, will make this gift flow into you so much more.

Don't pressure the ideas to come

There's a huge difference between ideas that come into your head spontaneously and organically versus pushing and forcing for an idea. You don't need to 'get' ideas, you just need to be clear enough for them to come to you. Bonus points if you don't get attached to any of them.

Differentiate who they're for

Sometimes the ideas that come are to do with you, your life, and your line of work, and other times, they're totally unrelated. To create the most success out of these ideas, start trying to tune in to which ones you think are for you to carry out and which ones are ideas that you can maybe give to others.

What Blocks This Gift

Doubting the validity or potential of these ideas

It's common for ideas people to think the ideas are silly, have no potential/aren't gonna go anywhere, or are 'unrealistic.'

So they start to think there's no point in doing anything about them.

What you need to know is that these ideas don't come from you, they come through you from Source. So even if you dismiss your *Self* as an unrealistic dreamer, these ideas don't come from that side of you – they are created by Source Energy/the Divine. There are millions of fully formed ideas surrounding us at all times, waiting for someone they can drop into, and your gift is to be a particularly good landing strip for them.

When you don't see the specialness of receiving ideas, you don't do anything with them. When you don't get these ideas out, they fester inside and create a blocked energy. Blocked energy then leads to fewer new ideas being dropped into you, and so you start to feel stagnant and uninspired.

Trust the images and concepts that come to you and know that they came to you for a reason. They are part of your service to the world.

Gift 12
The Capacity to Be Deeply Moved by Life

You are someone with an ability to be deeply moved by art and drama – both in creativity and in life.

But no matter how messy your life feels to you, others see you as moving through life in a charming, graceful way.

You are here to be deeply moved, by life and by art, and to transmit that to others – whether it's your laughter, your tears, your expression of how things make you feel. Words and actions get through to people so much more when there is heart connection behind them. We've been taught that that's a less respectable way to be than being stoic and unemotional, but you have to know that when you fully surrender to the drama, the highs and lows of your feelings, it is pure gold on you – and this grace and charm you're not even aware of is here to help others be attracted to you so that they can benefit from the wisdom of what you're expressing.

How to Flex This Gift

Wisdom, in your case, is not what you know – it's what you feel. There's no science or evidence to prove that what you're sharing is benefiting others, and you can't always see *how* it's benefiting others – especially not in the beginning when you don't think it has any value.

But know that most people are asleep in their lives because they *don't* feel – and when you *fully* feel, it helps them reconnect to their feelings, by getting a taste of it through you. You open up other people's emotional body. Your reactions to things may be more deep/extreme than others', but that's because it has to be strong enough to shake other people up.

You are someone who has the capacity and bravery to be fully changed by a song, a heartache, and that makes others feel more alive. It helps them open up their hearts too. That lightness is here to help the expressing of deep things not feel so daunting or heavy.

There is a purity to you, because you don't dull your reactions to suit society. You're still connected to the heart in a very pure way.

How you flex this gift is simply by removing any judgment about being this way. And when you see it as a beautiful gift, that will be reflected as strength in whatever you put into the world, which will make others more likely to gravitate toward you.

What Blocks This Gift

This part of you makes you so pure; but make sure that it doesn't convince your ego that you are purer, or more of a good person, than others. They have their own ways that they are connected to purity.

You can also have a judgment over being too 'all over the place' emotionally, because society values people who 'keep it all together.' Don't fall into that trap of being dulled by life. Be messy. Live in the emotions of life. Your sadness and your joy transform other people in a way that we so badly need. The journey into the heart is facilitated by people like you who are brave enough to put yours out into the world.

Gift 13
Listening and Collecting Stories

A person with Gift 13 is a great listener without even trying. And what's more, people feel totally at ease talking to you, or even confiding in you, without really knowing why they do.

Absorbing what you hear and collecting up people's stories, viewpoints, experiences, majorly informs what you put out into the world. What people say is quite literally your inspiration and your evidence.

Once you gather all this raw data, and it adds up, it starts to give you aha moments. You will notice threads, messages, or patterns that run through our experiences.

Next, you're meant to put that wisdom to good use. Whether those aha moments give you direction on what to create in technology, fashion, in your private practice – it doesn't matter. You turn personal anecdotes into universalized knowings or offerings that can serve many.

How to Flex This Gift

Truly absorb what people are saying instead of focusing on acting like a good listener

When you have true, objective, detached listening, you become a magnet for wisdom to come your way. The more open you are, the more comes to you, without you having to go get it. The less you feel the need to perform in conversation and just experience it, the more this gift will soar.

Picture literally soaking up what you hear and see and be open to whatever intel is contained underneath it, without agenda or need. Sometimes it will be that one thing you hear changes your whole direction, but most often it will be more passive than that, where the general practice of being open to people, their energy, connecting to their Essence, will upgrade your consciousness deeper and deeper – almost as a background activity in your everyday life.

How to Unblock This Gift

Do it with levity

Listening to others doesn't mean you carry the weight of their words and burdens. Nor does it mean you have a responsibility to tell them what's right or to fix them.

Sometimes people with this gift start to feel like listening to others, and therefore interacting with them in general, is hard work. It starts to feel heavy and draining, when it's meant to be part of how you come into your genius.

This will lead a person with Gift 13 to just 'go through the motions' of social interaction, maybe passively agreeing with everything other people say (or the other way, disagreeing and causing friction without reason), having a whole conversation(s) with people without actually giving or receiving anything. It's an interaction without exchange, without bonding. This cannot only numb a person's joy and connection out but also totally numb their gift.

Make a point to keep reminding yourself that you don't have to 'take on' people's words as truth, they are always subjective. You can listen without feeling like you have to validate or agree with people's narratives. Hear whatever you hear, but filter out whatever doesn't feel good to you.

If it helps, just think of their words as coming from Source, not from the people themselves, and Source is using people simply as the vehicles to help you get smarter and wiser. You'll feel lighter that way and less likely to be turned off by interaction as a whole.

Gift 14
Expanding What's Good in Others

Those with Gift 14 are adept at helping other people thrive and at creating prosperity for them, and doing this is also the surest route for creating abundance in their own lives.

If you have this gift, whoever you are (or have been) in an intimate relationship with likely became more successful while being with you

– same goes for the friends and family members whose bonds you put energy into and cherish. It's a simple rule for you that you will become most successful by devoting your life to helping create success for others – because that's what you're adept at.

How to Flex This Gift

Make it about serving others

Hone in on the specific ways you add value to others' lives, no matter how big or small, special or regular it sounds. Whatever you are good at increasing in others – do that. It could be their health, their wealth, their lifestyle, the system with which they sign a contract or make their coffee – each person with Gift 14 has an affinity with a different area of contributing to a good life.

So ask yourself which one(s) you naturally love to do? Usually it's the thing(s) that seems so obvious to you, that you probably do for free, without even noticing it's of value.

It's also important that you focus your intentions and energy on serving other people rather than think too much about how you're going to improve your own; the latter ironically happens best when you're focused on the former. And life will feel so much more fulfilling when expanding others' life experience is front and center of your intentions.

Lean in to your capable nature

The more you feel capable, confident in your abilities, and enthusiastic about using them – the more you'll create success all around you. This feeling is so contagious that all you've got to do is focus on cultivating it as much as possible in yourself, that anyone else you put energy into (whether directly or not, whether you know them personally or are just reaching them with something you're doing in the world) will be imbued with it too. You know you've really cultivated this feeling when you have this *knowing* that, no matter what comes your way, you'll be able to adapt and make something amazing out of it. When it feels so good to rely on yourself. When you love feeling independent and happy to radiate power – a power that we can all access. This gift is not about hierarchical power, it's about power that we all are privy to.

How to Unblock This Gift

Keep thinking bigger

It's likely you dreamed of big things from an early age, but often being a dreamer gets dismissed as naive or unrealistic. This stamps your gift out of you. The extent to which you feel disconnected to this gift is the extent to which you feel unconfident and unexcited by your own potential.

Your work with this gift is to clear any thoughts or conditioning that makes you feel *un*enthusiastic about life or *in*capable in your own abilities. Doubts and dispassion kill this gift.

Gift 15
Exploring the Edges

Have you ever felt drawn toward extremes or been called an extreme person? You're naturally quite fearless and will happily dive right into things because you have a need to explore, a need to go to the edges of what the spectrum is. You are the envoy for us all – you go explore something, understand it, and bring back the gifts or information. We all benefit from you venturing to places we won't lean into. You're the one to shine a light on these extremes for people, to show us that there's actually some good upsides of these edges that we could all maybe bring into our lives, without us needing to go to that extreme or learn those lessons ourselves. By you going to those extremes and then accepting them and learning the gifts from them, you can then bring them back as wisdom for everybody else. Being called 'extreme' is only bad if it's done out of foolishness. But when your Soul calls you there, it will always bring you gold. So don't be afraid to jump in with both feet.

How to Flex This Gift

Explore with an open mind

This gift really shines when it's done with a child's mind – open and curious to all the wonders the world could surprise and delight you with. So go without needing a certain outcome or finding, and be totally open to receive whatever the true finding is. This is how you'll glean real knowledge from your adventures: not having expectations before you start so that your consciousness is as wide open as it can be.

Realize there's no right and wrong

Pushing the limitations and norms sometimes helps us see new good things, and other times it reminds us why we need certain lines in the sand. Either way, you learn something that helps us live better. But you can be paralyzed to venture out if you're worried about 'doing life wrong' or making mistakes. Being more adventurous and unafraid will always make others a little fearful, which, if they don't know how to process it, they will project on you. But know this: if your heart is leading you there, you just can't get it wrong. There is no such thing as doing life wrong in an outside, measurable fashion. There is only doing right by your inner manual.

What Blocks This Gift

Going to the extreme for a reaction

Don't go or do radical things if it's to get a reaction from people, whether that's validation or to test your boundaries with them personally. The boundaries you want to test should always be your own. Venture into things you would do if no one was watching.

Gift 16
Enthusiasm

People with Gift 16 came here to be exceptionally enthusiastic people – especially when talking about things that light them up or rile them up.

This enthusiasm is connected to the throat in Human Design, so using your voice is an important part of you spreading your Purpose in this life.

Having this enthusiasm is like a booster that's here to help what you say really get through to people. It's like you've got an amplifier on what you say so that whatever you *do* choose to say really shakes people up and draws them toward you.

Deep down, you know that your voice has a powerful impact. Make sure you use it authentically. You don't have to *try* to make an impact, it's something that will naturally happen when you're speaking about what things make you passionate. So don't go out of your way to shake people or say controversial things on purpose – if those are masterminded, people will feel that, and it will turn them off. So for example, don't talk about the current hot topic because you think that's what impactful, passionate people *should* talk about; talk about whatever it is you are jazzed by in that very moment.

How to Flex This Gift

Let your passions roam

Spread your skills, your interest, and your curiosity far and wide. Don't limit yourself to one box, because you're not meant to. With this gift, you can become good at anything you're genuinely drawn to. Usually, people with this gift get involved in culture and the arts in some way.

How to Unblock This Gift

Remove apathy

Look at all the areas of your life where you are approaching things apathetically. Where do you feel yourself just going through the motions rather than showing up jazzed? See your feelings toward life as a top priority, all along your journey through life, because that's what will improve the value of whatever comes out of you. Your enthusiasm and positivity increases the value in everything you do.

Also, know that enthusiasm isn't always viewed by others as 'cool' – because of our conditioning that being stoic and reserved is better. Many have dulled their excitement for life because cultivating this non-feeling, nonchalant air is revered by our society. Make sure this doesn't ever make you want to do the same, or ever make you feel like you're 'too much' for others. Shine on. Once they see your way is actually much more fun, you might end up converting them anyway; but either way, you'll be enjoying your own experience of life to the max.

Gift 17
A Fair, Methodical Mind

A person with Gift 17 has a very strong left brain.

We call this a scientist's mind because the way they understand life is very fair and methodical – you don't just 'make up' what you want to be true. You look at all the evidence, sift through it with a keen eye, and from there, it's easy for you to tell what the Truth is. What's more, you can back up this truth with facts, because you've built your knowings on solid foundations.

How to Flex This Gift

See the value it brings

We need this gift in today's world more than ever. Most people decide what they want to be true first and *then* look for any evidence that will prove they're right, without looking at the whole picture (this is known as confirmation bias).

At their best, people with your gift are much more open-minded than that. Ideally on any subject that calls you to delve into it, you approach it without pre-deciding the answer. You remove any personal agendas and allow the truth to show itself to you – through the numbers, the words, the studies, the facts – whatever it is.

The thing about truth though, is that it's revealed to us in layers. On one level for example, time is linear. On a higher level of understanding, it doesn't exist. Both are technically 'true.' For you, it's most important that you don't attach yourself to current or previous conclusions and truths you arrived at, because that will block you from seeing things in an even higher way. Truth is not a final destination, it reveals itself deeper and deeper the more we make ourselves ripe to receive it. Keep a totally open and detached mind. Remain a forever student.

What Blocks This Gift

Needing our findings to be final

Sometimes we would prefer to see truth as a final destination because it feels safe. It allows our ego to construct a fixed view of reality if it feels it already knows 'all the facts.' But you *never* have all the facts. The more you feel comfortable about that, and in fact excited to keep learning and understanding higher, the more you'll strengthen this gift.

How to Unblock This Gift

When you've opened your mind, open it some more

Your practice is to keep challenging the places where you have closed your mind. Ask yourself: Where are you holding on to a fixed way of seeing things? Like where in your life are you *so* sure things work *this* way? Is there any possibility you can challenge yourself to see that there might be different sides to it, different truths?

Remember the rarity of this gift. Because scientific discovery has been created by using the process that's natural to you, we assume that everybody has a mind that works this way. This is not the case. Understand that having a mind like this is of real value because it's the only way we uncover new levels of understanding about how our world works.

When you understand it's unusual, you see the potential value-add in it, and then you can go act on it.

Don't assume others have the same capability of fairness and openness as you and keep challenging your*self* to new levels of fairness and openness.

Gift 18
Questioning Authority

Gift 18 has an intuitive ability to tell who and what is in their integrity and who is not. They are unafraid to look at anyone, no matter their titles and status, and discern their conduct.

Gift 18 doesn't care about the job titles or the positions. It cares if you're being a good human and acting in your own Alignment. If your actions match up to your values. It cares about what can be made better, no matter where you are on the journey.

You have naturally high standards of conduct and are here to hold everyone up to the mark.

There are many examples of us all doing this in a harsh, judgmental way, but for you, you are here to do it with heart. You are here to find a way of using your critical eye so that it truly helps people and serves us all as a whole. This is not about judging people and dismissing them or writing them off as 'bad.' This is about seeing where they're living up to their potential and where they're not, because we all need see-ers to help us realign. We can't all see ourselves so clearly all of the time.

We also need see-ers to look at the people with authority and discern how well they're showing up.

We're living in a time where anyone in a position of power who's not acting kindly and correctly won't be able to stay in their position for long. There has never been a more important time to let this gift shine.

How to Flex This Gift

See everyone as just a human being

This gift will strengthen the more you see that no one is untouchable or 'above' you. Nor are they below you.

We've all been taught to constantly assess whether people are above or below, better or worse, stronger or weaker than us, and for you, it's especially important that you dissolve these constructs in the way you see the world – so that there is one standard you hold everyone up to, no matter who they are or what their capabilities are.

Reframe flaws

Having flaws doesn't disqualify or dismiss anyone – and when you can apply your discernment with this true acceptance of our shared humanness, it creates a whole new paradigm of how we improve as people. Make it so that any and all imperfections you may spot are just opportunities for more Light to be created.

What Blocks This Gift

The compulsion to fix everyone

People with this gift can spend way too much time judging and criticizing others, whether that's out loud or just silently, and it only brings both sides down. Just because you *can* see how things can be made better, you don't want to use this ability when it's feeding your ego and insecurities. Trying to fix and change others, believing they should bend to how *you* think they should be, is an addiction of the mind that will only deplete you and leak that gift in places which won't be fruitful. Reserve your gift for times and places where there's no emotional charge or agenda from your side.

Gift 19
Sensing People's Needs

Having Gift 19 gives you an effortless ability to tap into what people need to survive and thrive.

On the most basic level, this means sensing their physical needs – for food, for touch, and for a home. And then, also our emotional and spiritual needs – for community, for belonging, and for a connection to Spirit.

Your Purpose in life is to help provide something(s) that falls into at least one of these categories for other people, whether directly or indirectly. You can see and feel what we collectively need, what will serve our well-being and our evolution, and you can give it to us or guide us toward it.

On a literal level, the spiritual and material planes are separate, but eventually your work will bring the two together in some way. Ultimately, there isn't one without the other. The more you see Spirit in the physical, rather than this thing so far removed and above us, the better.

How to Flex This Gift

Be your own first try

Usually, your journey to taking care of your own physical, emotional, and spiritual needs will guide you right toward what you'll end up providing for others.

So take a look at your life, both in your early years and now, and think of where you feel a need is missing, times when you craved for a basic need but didn't receive it. The pain of feeling the lack of something is nudging you to learn how to give it to yourself, almost as your own guinea pig, so that you can then share it with others.

The Universe made you extra sensitized, to your environment, to things you take in, to other people's subconscious, to aid you with this gift, this ability to feel energetic nuances so deeply. So often people with this gift need to be extra choosy or intentional about what they consume.

And the same is true for energetic consumption as what they consume physically; as they tune in more and more, they feel extra turned off by their own negative behavior so that it really grabs their attention – because there is always a clue in there about how society in general behaves and what the cure is.

There is no limit to how deep this gift can go – at higher levels it can mean you receive visions in dreams, see beyond the fabric of physical reality, and become psychic.

How to Unblock This Gift

Don't let codependency run the show

The ability to sense other people's needs so easily can amplify codependent tendencies. Think about it – you know exactly what people need, and your Soul is always inclined to tap into it. So it's extremely easy for you to use this skill to get validation, love, or approval from others.

But using it on this drains it from being used in other parts of your life – parts that will actually serve and elevate so many, including you.

The less you depend on others for validation, and the more independent you become emotionally, meeting all of your own Higher needs, the more you will receive guidance on how to elevate society.

Gift 20

Happy-Go-Lucky

Those with Gift 20 are here to be naturally trusting in Life. When you believe that Life is a joy and that things usually work out for the greater good, you can feel relaxed because you know you don't need to be controlling everything for things to go well.

You're aware that there are unseen forces at work, whether you call that God, the Universe, or Spirit.

And so this brings a certain lightness to your being. You can bring humor; you can smile through the regular every day, *and* through challenging times, because you know not to take it all so seriously. You know that we're just here for a short ride, and that perspective is a key part of your energy.

This energy is connected to the Throat in Human Design, and so this hopeful, light perspective is usually spread to others with what you say. Gift 20 people tend to be great storytellers and raconteurs, or they just share their positive outlook on life.

How to Flex This Gift

Call it as it is

In order to be truly in this gift, you need to be unafraid to tell things as they are – and first to yourself. Because you tend toward the positive, sometimes looking at the unpleasant stuff can feel especially jarring or scary to you. But it's only by looking at it *all* that you'll discover that, *even* through the negative parts of life, you're a person who still has that deep trust in Life supporting you. You can't truly know that if you only look at the already-positive things.

By leaning into darkness, you will see how Light you really are. In fact, you also can turn the dark parts into humor and positivity for others. Some with this gift are great comedians because they have a deep grasp for the silliness of life; they see the funny side when so many of us are stuck in the seriousness.

How to Unblock This Gift

Don't force yourself into performative happiness

When we are Happy Go Lucky at a shallow level, we paint over everything (including our pain) by cultivating a saccharine or fake happiness. We go overboard with positivity, or we overcompensate when anything slightly negative comes up. We might feel the need to reassure everyone who is feeling anything but 100 percent upbeat.

A deeper Happy Go Lucky is based on allowing yourself to feel everything you authentically feel, and then noticing that 'Wow, my general tendency is toward trust – trust that everything is going to be okay. Now I can relax. Now I don't have to overcompensate or hide the negatives.' That deeper way is your gift. It's here to show others that we don't need to worry as much as we do. We don't need to take things as heavy or seriously as we do. But in order to spread this gift, you need to be okay with any negative feelings you have that come up. You need to get to that place where you know they're not the end-all be-all for yourself. Only then can you remind others of this Truth too.

Gift 21
Cultivating Personal Power

Gift 21 is a person who is meant to take charge, both of themselves and others.

Taking charge of your own life primarily means you came here to become financially independent and abundant. It's *healthy* for people with Gift 21 to be motivated by money because it's part of your path in this life – to give yourself every material thing you could want.

It also means that you need to feel very in charge with the choices you make for your own lifestyle, whether that's with your wardrobe, your environment, your food choices, etc. These are not silly endeavors for you, they are part of you learning to master the material plane, which is part of what you came here to do.

In coming into feeling powerful yourself, you can help others do the same.

You also have an energy that radiates assertion and self-assuredness, which makes others happy to receive your direction.

How to Flex This Gift

Get comfortable taking charge

People with this gift are very comfortable directing other people, because that's what they're here to do.

If you hate being told what to do by others, this isn't bad – it's the way you're designed! Your lesson in this life is learning to become your *own* boss, so Life is going to make taking other people's direction very unpleasant for you.

If you don't feel comfortable directing others, ask yourself what negative associations or fears you have about being in a powerful position. Understand that when done with good consciousness, it can only benefit other people. Directing others doesn't put you 'above' them, it puts you in their service. When you see your role of power as the ultimate act of service, those discomforts of being in charge will dissolve.

What Blocks This Gift

Control

The negative side of taking charge is being controlling. In the areas of life where you become obsessive, compulsive, superstitious, or controlling of other people, these are when you're using the gift in the wrong places and for the wrong things. The gift should be used to feel more sovereign and free over your own life and to guide others toward the same thing.

Use this gift of directing people in the specific areas where you have value to give and refrain from telling them how to live their whole life.

Your ego will push you to do the latter, because it will tell you you have all the answers. And your fear will tell you you are safer when you're micromanaging everything. The antidote to this is to always return to the intention of service. To your duty and responsibility to steer a ship for other people, with humility and a pure heart. That is who you are at the core.

Gift 22
Emotional Modeling

These people have been given the gift of deep emotional capacity – they can feel the highest of highs, the lowest of lows, and everything in between.

Most people don't have access to such a huge spectrum of feeling, unless something extreme happens to them in their lives, whereas you can feel extremely happy from something that would make most people just 'happy.' And you can also be more deeply affected by something saddening. What is borne from this level of feeling is deep empathy, inspiration, and creativity.

How to Flex This Gift

When you're in a high mood, you are extremely magnetic to other people and love to socialize. You come across as charming and graceful without even trying, and people can't get enough of you. You are here to transmit these magnified highs in those moments, which elevates other people because they don't normally have access to these high states, and it's through people like you that they even get a chance to touch them.

As for the lows, you can't have the Highest of highs without them. Usually, people think they're doing something 'wrong' when they feel a low. This is not true! Your moods are given to you so you can develop your emotional intelligence.

Instead of letting your mind get lost in trying to analyze or judge yourself or others for it, you're here to find freedom from it. To realize that your feelings aren't these heavy hard things that control you.

This is an integral gift of yours. To free yourself from the hold emotions have over you and in turn free others too. We need to realize that emotions are just experiences, neither positive or negative, and since you have access to more of them, you are a teacher on how the whole spectrum works.

How to Unblock This Gift

See it with levity

Once you remove the shame and the stigma from negative emotions, you allow all emotions to be gifts – for they contain intel and wisdom that we're meant to benefit from.

When you accept the lows for what they are (just an experience that you can choose to neutrally observe and glean insight from), you can unlock huge amounts of empathy, because you know how people going through lows feel.

When you're in a high, spread it far and wide. The Universe has given you that specific high because it's time to get out and to shine.

When you're in a low, retreat. This is the Universe's way of saying this is a time to go inward. Let the bluesiness, the sadness, or the depression pass without taking it to mean too much.

The key is to remember that your emotions don't say anything about how good or bad you are: they are transitory, just like the weather. If you identify with them, they will hang around longer, which can cause prolonged states of low moods. If you don't take them to mean anything personal about you, they will pass like the clouds.

Once you've done this enough, and you've mastered freedom from letting these low moods control you, you are here to model that for others so that they can do the same.

No matter how roller-coaster-y your life feels to you internally, you will transform that into grace and charm when you allow it to be what it is. This is the magic of Gift 22 – showing us how to move through all our human states of happiness and sadness with grace.

Gift 23
Clarity

Gift 23 has the gift of expressing things in a clear, direct way. And what you're here to express are new perspectives and approaches to things. You don't come to these perspectives in a strategic way nor by being logical or by being a dreamer; you simply sit back with a receptive, uncluttered mind to contemplate a situation, and then at a certain point a 'knowing' drops in. All of a sudden, you get clarity. This clarity is utterly ahead of its time and so needed by others because they are flashes of insight that can bring giant leaps of advancement to any areas of the human experience you're passionate about.

You tend toward being practical and efficient, so these are usually also signature markers of the solutions and upgrades you bring to the table.

This process makes you an original and lateral thinker because this clarity doesn't have a set process – you just 'know things' without knowing where they came from or how you got to them. Resist the urge to explain what you say or that you need a logical process for it to be valid and valuable.

Trust that inner knowing that gets delivered to you; and be in service to it by sharing it with others.

The second part of this gift, which is the part that other people notice, is the directness in the way you deliver this insight. Directness is intense because it hits you like a lightning bolt – it leaves no uncertainty or confusion in what's been said. But directness doesn't have to mean serious or harsh – it's at its best when it's both clear and light, even humorous at times.

How to Flex This Gift

When you have this gift, your role is to clear your mind as much as possible. Not to chase and force clarity but to prep yourself to receive clarity as much as possible. Society praises us for saying 'smart things,' so sometimes we can try and force ourselves to say things or have an answer on stuff, whether for ourselves or for an audience, before our minds are truly, organically ready.

Doing so not only clutters the brain with the premature and, therefore, not 'real' clarity, pushing out space for the true clarity to come in when it wants to. But it also throws you out of Divine Timing, because when you force clarity, it will usually make you take action around that clarity, and thus, do something that isn't actually Aligned for you. When we act this way, like surer and sooner is always better, we can end up taking a disproportionate amount of action to get results we desire, spinning our wheels unnecessarily and wasting our precious Life Force.

From a physical standpoint, you can also flex this gift by making your space feel conducive to clarity – whether that's an uncluttered home, if that helps you think better, or surrounding yourself with possessions that feel like a reflection of your best you.

What Blocks This Gift

Being too polite or nice, watching your words so as not to offend people

Remember that directness and utter clarity are your strengths, especially when delivered with lightness. Don't water down your genius for anything or anyone.

Trying to explain yourself too much or overcomplicating your communication

This usually comes from the belief that people don't understand us; which then leads us to over explain, which also loses people's attention, and so confirming the belief. Try choosing less words and trusting that the right people, people who get you and are on your frequency, will not only receive them, but receive them deeply, because you have let your insights flow straight through you from the Divine, totally unfettered.

Gift 24
Quiet Breakthroughs

If you have Gift 24, you have the ability to constantly upgrade your understanding of life to higher dimensions.

You know that saying 'Problems cannot be solved at the same level of thinking that created them'? That's you, Gift 24. Transcending your current approach so you can 'see' more clearly and consciously.

You are someone who is always reaching for more clarity in your life – whether that's a situation you're in, or a subject you're interested in. And you have the patience to ponder, ponder, ponder that same thing – until one day, all of a sudden, poof – clarity comes. You get an aha moment.

Pondering is more passive than thinking – you're not forcing the answer, you're just giving it time in your brain and staying open, ready to receive the clarity whenever the perfect time is for you to receive it.

How to Flex This Gift

Don't think more, think better

Aha moments happen when you improve the *quality* of your thinking. Essentially, you don't need to think *more*, you just need to think better, and you're someone who is so skilled at this.

Most of us think about the same handful of things on repeat, day in, day out. And in the same patterns. For the average person, thinking about thought A always leads them to think thought B. This person might feel like they're *choosing* each of their thoughts, but they're actually dictated by their hardwiring.

You, Gift 24, can hotwire this hardwiring. You can observe your automatic thought patterns and bust out of them, creating entirely new ones. Ones that you've actually chosen and that serve you.

A person with Gift 24 has that huge capacity to rise up above these patterns and experience new ways of thinking. This is because you have a highly original mind that can see above the mental chatter that rules most people's minds. In doing so – you are here to move us forward and help bring in healthier, better relationships to our thought processes. This is a big part of your Purpose here.

You are here to transcend regular ways of thinking and push your mind to higher levels of understanding. When you do – you have breakthroughs in the way you see. It's like wearing a better pair of glasses all of a sudden: what you're looking at doesn't change, but your perspective has been upgraded.

What Blocks This Gift

Filling your mind with distractions or staying busy

It's in the silence and doing nothing that your life gets changed. Most of your genius and most of your growth will come when you remove all the unnecessary stimulation and activity.

Forcing an answer rather than staying open for it

The beauty of this gift is in having that 'open to receive' state. Even though the world will tell you that you do, you don't have to have an answer for everything, all the time. The best truths and answers are the ones we water carefully with our time and attention, but we allow to bloom when they're ready. Plus, having positive forward movement in our lives is not about having more answers, it's about having better answers.

Realize that not everyone has this same patience and openness to breakthroughs as you do

Sometimes, we overlook what could be so valuable, simply because we don't realize it is. And if we don't realize it, we don't flex it and put it to use. Only when we do, does it have the chance to flower.

Gift 25
Embracing Life with Childlike Innocence

No matter whether you're eight or 80, people will always see you as being 'young' in your energy. Beneath this is a freshness and a zest for life, which has the incredible power to revive and rejuvenate the world. For most people, life feels more and more heavy the longer they live it. This is the cause of 'aging': getting too weighed down and humdrum about life, without looking at things with excitement and wonder, sucks the life out of people. Your Lightness can bring them back to life.

Your job is to strengthen that fresh approach to life in yourself first and spread it far and wide. Let it bleed into everything you do, whether that's human resources or singing – it doesn't matter.

The Buddhists talk about the highest wisdom being 'the Child's mind,' which is essentially seeing everything with fresh eyes, as if for the first time. Not getting jaded and familiar. Our culture has taught us the opposite: that being nonchalant and 'realistic' is good and smart. That excitement is silly and frivolous. But the ultimate wisdom is preserving that light spiritedness and seeing life as the joy and gift that it is. You are here to show us how this childlike spirit *and* being in your power can not only go together but also enhance each other.

How to Flex This Gift

Reframe it as strength

This gift is at its peak when you start to see it as real strength. When the world throws you many reasons to build up walls and close your heart down, but you stay open. When you are loving and pure, without thinking that means you need to be a pushover or to people-please. The sweet spot is saying how you feel and saying what you want, but always in a light and kind way. If others see you as naive, let them. If others mistake this innocence as an opportunity to take advantage, they'll soon find out they were wrong.

Keep your joy and purity no matter what

Always come back to your innocence. Don't let the world or others stamp that beautiful innocence out of you. They're the ones that need to become more like you, not the other way round. You will always feel most secure and comfortable when you come back to your home base, this open light spirit of yours. Whenever you are lost or off track, know you can always come back.

What Blocks This Gift

Playing it cool

Getting 'serious' about any areas of life because we've been told we need to in order to become successful. Success and light heartedness are not mutually exclusive, and after all, what's the point of making all your dreams come true if you're unable to be in joy while having them?

Gift 26
Knowing the Right Way to Say Things

A person with Gift 26 has great interpersonal skills. It knows how to get through to people. It knows how to get a message across in a way that will sound good or resonate. In this way, having this gift makes you the ultimate sales person, presenting people with things they need and delivering it in a way that will engage their desires. Sometimes we don't know what we want before it gets presented in a way that we connect to, and this is what you're here to do.

This gift also comes with incredible efficiency, which means you are always driven to do the minimum effort for the maximum result. You like to cut the pfaff and take the most direct route. This is not laziness, this is smarts – the whole world is becoming more efficient, and having this knack to cut corners and get things done quicker can bring incredible value to others (as well as to your own process of getting things done, of course).

There's a healthy dose of desire and motivation to this gift too: your Soul came to create success, for yourself and for your tribe. It's good for you to embrace these true desires of yours and follow them. You want everyone to have the best.

How to Flex This Gift

Put the things you're passionate about on the center stage of your life

The more you care deeply about the things you're sharing with others, the more this gift will activate – without you having to really sell in the cliché way – people will just want in on your passionate energy. You'll be a great communicator and spreader of your message, your product, or your service, without having to figure out 'how' to do it. People have all sorts of tricks and complicated strategies regarding the art of selling – but you're here to show that it's best done when done from a true love for something. Follow your heart's desires, and people will want whatever it is you're offering.

What Blocks This Gift

Shame or fear about being passionate

Sometimes we're afraid to sing our passions from the rooftops because they're an extension of our Souls, so we don't want people criticizing, questioning, or rejecting them. Or we think that being passionate and fiery is negative because 'Who do we think we are?' We've been taught it's better to be cool and stoic. It's better to not care.

But the world is desperate for people who have come all the way alive and are out and happy to let it pour out of them. Our spirits need passionate people more than we need what they're actually passionate about – because that passion has the power to connect *us* to the energy of passion too.

Sometimes people will want whatever it is you're passionate about just because being part of your Lit up energy lifts them up. It's not the products; it's how the experience of those products make us feel – and it starts with you.

The intentions behind it

Sometimes we associate selling, persuading, and sharing with being manipulative and taking advantage of people. But when you approach it with the consciousness of helping others discover and connect to things that will improve their life experience, it's a whole different beast. The old way is benefiting from other people's loss; the new way is win-win. When you show up to share, do it from an intention of service, and people will feel that from you, magnetizing them to you even more. Everybody feels energy whether they know it or not, and they'll gravitate so much more to authentic passion rather than 'selling' that has been manufactured or overly formulated, schemed, or thought through.

Gift 27
A Natural Affinity for Nurture and Care

Taking care of other people comes naturally to you. You might think, 'Doesn't everyone care about other people?' And the answer is no, not to the extent that you do. Care and nurture is your superpower.

The issue with that superpower is that society doesn't place a high value on that – so you probably don't see the high value in this part of you either. You probably didn't hear anyone ever tell you that your incredible ability to care would make you a bajillionaire, or a president. But now more than ever, when we can accumulate pretty much as many material possessions as we want, what people desire more than ever is to feel this care. When you infuse this care into everything you do, whether that's being a mom or being in charge of a big brand, is when you'll find the most success. When you lead with how much you care for people and let that bleed into everything you do, that's what will make people gravitate toward you the most.

How to Flex This Gift

Include yourself in your care

The main lesson for people with this gift is learning to balance how much energy you put into taking care of others versus balancing that with taking care of your Self too. This gift of nurturing, like all gifts, has to be applied to all areas of life in order for it to fully flourish, so if you neglect yourself, you will never truly access the fruits that are on the other side of this gift.

Let your care shine

Let how much you care be felt. Everything that tugs at your heart is sacred – pledge allegiance to it above all and don't apologize for it – show it off! People are so magnetized to people who give an eff in this world, because it's passion. It's aliveness. It's love. It's all the things we want more of in our own lives. When they feel that coming off of you, it's like a stream that makes it easier for them to get to those things in themselves too.

What Blocks This Gift

Thinking of caring for people as a duty, which starts to make it feel heavy, when, really, your care is meant to be your joy and your pleasure, a physical expression of your love. Make sure you do it in a way that is enjoyable for you. Just because you care and adore people, doesn't mean you should enslave yourself.

Letting guilt or helplessness drive your actions

People with this gift often feel guilt that they're not doing enough, fear that they can't do enough, or helplessness over the fact that what they did didn't get the results or reach they wanted it to. These kinds of thoughts are poor fuel for your care; whereas when your care is from feeling it in your heart and not being able to help letting it show, it's a whole other level of gift people are getting from any one action you take.

It also doesn't mean you should be doing everything for everyone. Do the caring things that excite you and remember care is an energy as well as an act. You don't have to be 'doing' all the time.

Doing it too much will drain and deplete you, making you bitter toward the people you're sharing your heart with. This removes any positive effects you'd be transfusing into people, which is the whole point anyway. Trust in doing what Lights you up, and trust in the value of it.

Gift 28

Maximizing Life

Gift 28 is fixated with making the most out of life, wanting to ensure that they live it to the fullest and squeeze every last bit of juice out of what it has to offer. This is because a humdrum life is not for you.

And life has made you dread that, to ensure you keep reaching for higher heights of what you can make of this Life.

This gift is here to drive you toward excellence and push you out of any limits that are restricting you, because you came here to live a big life.

The irony is that most limitations on us living life to the full come from ourselves. In a bid to get the most out of life, Gift 28s often have an overwhelming fear of running out of time or 'being behind' in life, or sometimes even of dying before their time. This leads to constant impatience, always feeling rushed, or overly routine-ing your life – all of which actually *prevent* you from manifesting that greatness you're here to. All of these are fears and anxieties, which constrict your energy and block your full access to lateral thinking and creative solutions. You're putting yourself and your life on to this 'track,' which is restricting your Spirit. And your Spirit is the part of you that, when free, can get you there fastest.

Once you remove all this pressure that's controlling the actions you take in your day, it's like taking the blinders off, and you can suddenly see and think more clearly, which means you create bigger, better stuff.

Pressure and rushing is fear-based energy; being intentional about everything you do and being present to it is a bigger, more powerful energy to be in.

How to Flex This Gift

What you need to realize is that pressuring and rushing through life is *not* living it to the full. Sure, you can go through the motions of what we've been told creates a good life, but if you're not taking it in, your life will actually pass by faster (or seem to) than if you pay attention to what's right in front of you, what you're doing now, and use your wonderful gift to create the best, most enjoyable experience out of every moment or situation.

So start from a blank slate: figure out what living a full life means to you. And then let the way you spend your time and attention revolve around that. We all have different versions of this, and society definitely has its cookie-cutter idea too. Getting clear on *your* visions, feelings, or thoughts around your life will help you direct your actions so that you actually create what you want.

What Blocks This Gift

Performing your daily activities rather than engaging in them. When you engage, there are messages. Maybe you'll realize you don't actually enjoy one of them and come up with an alternative. This is a superpower: to be able to upgrade and improve the enjoyment of things. But you can't do that if you're treating yourself like a robot and forcing yourself to just 'get on with it' because of where you think it's going to lead you. You can't get to happiness if you don't cultivate it on the way there.

Gift 29
Being 'All In'

When you say yes to something, Gift 29, you're all in on it. The energy of this gift is about throwing your full power and energy into everything you do.

When you feel excitement about something, it sparks a force inside you that will create momentum in whatever that project or activity is.

This is a force that really can move mountains in the world, and this is the gift that being 'all in' brings – forward movement, for your Self and for others.

There's also a trust element in this gift – you can go all in on something without needing to know exactly what will come of it. Your physical excitement is much more powerful than all the reasoning and rationalizing that your brain will try to get you to listen to instead.

What's more, your commitment to staying with something even if it 'doesn't make sense' or gets challenging, because you feel drawn to it without knowing why, has the ability to actually transform the situation for the better, no matter how undesirable or uncomfortable it may seem at times. Once you're invested in it, and truly from a place of excitement, it will turn into a more attractive situation to everyone else – whether that's work projects, objects, or people you bring into your life. Whatever you put your energy into suddenly looks like a great prospect in other people's eyes.

The lesson here is that passion conquers all. And it's also the powerful force that upgrades whatever you funnel it into.

How to Flex This Gift

Discerning between what's actually a yes for you and what's actually not that exciting to you

The more you only commit to things that light you up, the more each thing will be filled with passion and momentum. They will be the fuel that carries all your endeavors forward without you having to push and force it to become successful.

When you are 'all in' on something, it galvanizes others to come together and create forward movement, the kind that turns dreams into reality.

What Blocks This Gift

Committing to things you don't actually feel excited by

If you do, you'll inevitably overextend yourself and end up depleted. Try to look at the reasons you give yourself for saying yes to those things in the first place; usually, it will have come from the mind trying to convince you something was going to bring you results you wanted, with no regard to whether the process of getting it was actually enjoyable.

Being casual or nonchalant about things

This is so not your true nature, and anywhere in your life where you feel you have this attitude will bring misalignment. Connect to your passionate and committed Self and don't shrink that power in order to be more acceptable, more cool, or less threatening in society's eyes.

Gift 30
The Desire to Feel Deeply

Those with Gift 30 are always desiring big life experiences – the kind that make you fully feel alive, whether that's pleasurable or painful – they just desire to feel *something*, and they find themselves longing for more than what they're currently experiencing to give them that aliveness.

For some, this will show up as being an adrenaline junkie, for others it will be subtler life experiences, or movies and music. Most often though, Gift 30 is game for anything and wants to experience it all. It doesn't matter what you do, as long as it's authentic to you.

The purpose of this gift is to remind yourself and others of the joy of experience for experience's sake. This life can be a playground if we want it to be, and experiences are neither good nor bad, ultimately – they are just things we want to live out. There is a lightness to this gift because you let things be as they are and don't bear the weight of things that have happened to you, but you still soak up all the wisdom and lessons they were meant to give you. This is what this desire to feel deeply ensures happens to you. With Gift 30 you can be shaped by experiences more deeply than someone else going through the exact thing, and that's part of your Purpose.

How to Flex This Gift

Let go of any expectations you have when going into a new experience, whether that's a job, a relationship, or just a fun excursion. The more you can go into it with a totally open mind, the more you can embrace this gift of allowing every experience to fully move you and mold you in the way it's meant to. Expectations narrow the field of outcomes, whereas you want to blow that field wide open and allow the best possibilities to unfold for you.

What Blocks This Gift

Sometimes you can have this burning desire, but you don't know what for exactly. Like you have this fire inside of you but no clarity on what to do with it. It helps in this case not to pressure yourself to have the big answer, but just to start throwing yourself into little things that seem exciting to you. This helps you build trust in yourself to discern what experiences are right for you and which ones aren't.

Gift 31
Influential Energy

Gift 31 is effortlessly influential over the people around you. You have a certainty in the way you speak, and you project out an air that makes others want to listen to you, do what you do, or try things you recommend. You come across as a strong, self-assured person, which makes other people feel drawn to you.

In whatever role(s) you find yourself in life, you will find people want to follow you in some way. They will come to you for recommendations or suggestions because they trust your preferences. This gift plays a big part in your purpose on this Earth and requires you to not follow society, but to become someone that society wants to follow.

How to Flex This Gift

Let yourself like what you like

Get really into the things that grab your interest; own your likes and dislikes. Since you're meant to be an influential person, you can't allow your personal interests to be dictated by what most people are into. You will affect the status quo, not the other way round. So be original, be true to you, and allow yourself to like the things you like. It's all for a reason.

The more you can become your own person, self-assured and self-directed, the stronger you'll become as a force in the world.

Be unafraid to show your strength

Somehow, we've come to believe that influential or powerful people are 'better' than people who aren't. And for as long as our mentality accepts these beliefs, that's what energy people will feel behind our actions.

So yes, there are influential people who misuse their ability. But don't be afraid to embrace this power of yours, because you can do it in a *good*, *kind* way. You can do it with grace and with the intention of serving.

Sometimes, these societal beliefs make us shy away from showing up so self-assured – *or* it makes us exert it disproportionately. Being unafraid to show your strength is simply letting it come out of you without trying to make it be anything other than what it is. Own what you are sure of. When you do, you become a beacon for others to find their own strength too.

Being influential doesn't mean being better than others; it just means that you've been put in charge of bringing things to people's attention. It *is* a huge responsibility, though, because you have to make sure you do it with integrity, thinking and speaking and being only the things that are the highest standard you can at the time. So it is a position of power to that extent. It just doesn't make you 'more' powerful than others. Sometimes, this can trip people up because they can misuse this influence, *or* they can shy away from embracing their influential nature, because they believe they'd alienate or threaten other people if they were in their full power. Neither is true. Embrace your influence with a consciousness of doing it to serve others.

What Blocks This Gift

Doing things with the intention of influencing others

Since this gift is effortless, it can't be planned out; your influence actually becomes *less* powerful when you do things and say things for a given effect or result.

Gift 32
Having a Nose for Success

People with Gift 32 have a sixth sense for what's gonna work out and what isn't. Maybe you have a nose for what businesses will be successful, or a sense for whether a relationship will go the distance – this gift can show up in many ways. It's here to help guide and steer what you invest your time and energy into.

This skill is not based in logic or facts. It's a strong instinct/sixth sense, and you often can't explain *why* you feel things will be successful or not – in fact, when you can't explain why you feel this, it's a *good* sign because you're letting that pure instinct speak rather than letting your brain get in the way.

Gift 32 people show a healthy sense of restraint when putting money or energy into things, because they obviously won't invest in things they don't sense will be successful.

If you have this gift, it's here to guide your own actions and decisions, but also for you to steer others toward succeeding too. You can use this gift to help make others successful by using your Design's Strategy.

How to Flex This Gift

The thing about instinct is it doesn't speak to you always, in every situation – it will just speak up when it wants to. You don't have to push yourself to have all the answers for everything; you just need to open-mindedly listen out for that little whisper that will say, 'This feels right,' or 'Something feels off.' Everyone with this gift will have different areas of life that this gift will speak up in – whether that's investing in stocks, discerning what clients are right to collaborate with, relationship counseling.

What Blocks This Gift

A fear of failure

Since they are strongly oriented toward success, the biggest fear of Gift 32s is just the opposite – that they will fail.

This can show up in several different ways.

- Some people with this gift will be so afraid to fail that they are paralyzed to make any moves toward their dreams.

- Some are taking action, but out of fear rather than excitement.
- Others just think about failure for way too big a portion of their time.

Either way, you have to flip this on its head and understand that this nose for failure is here to help propel you to success when you get out of your head, don't listen to the fear, and make moves toward your dreams while always listening out for that little instinct that's here to guide you.

Gift 33
Going Within

At the surface level, people with this gift are people who need a lot of alone time.

But there's a much deeper reason to it; they are people whose life path leads them to shut off the noise from the outside world and connect to all the forces and things in this world that *can't* be seen.

For you, your genius is accessed from going inward, not by looking for it outwards.

Usually, this genius expresses and shares itself through writing, speaking, or teaching.

People with this gift are always looking for the deeper meaning and message behind something, because that's the wisdom they're here to find on behalf of the collective and share it with other people.

Sometimes, the fact that they spend so much time going within can make a person with Gift 33 feel very alone or cut off from the world. This is why them sharing their findings with others not only helps the recipients but helps them, too, because it draws them out into the world and brings them connection. A happy life for a person deep in this gift is a healthy balance of time spent discovering within and time spent getting out of themselves and sharing that new-found wisdom with others.

How to Flex This Gift

Don't feel guilty about your need for downtime – understand that it's how you access your other gifts and insights

So Disconnect. Unplug. Recharge. You need a lot of downtime and rest, and not just because everybody deserves relaxation, but also because what happens during that time adds such value to the actual 'doing' you do in this life.

What Blocks This Gift

Taking lots of downtime, but filling it with stimulation

There's nothing you really have to 'do' to connect to your genius other than make yourself available for it to come to you. But for most of us, when we take downtime, we're watching TV, scrolling our phones, or just still busying our minds. The type of downtime that will really serve your genius is the downtime where you literally stare at the wall, or the stars: a totally empty mind. Try taking yourself somewhere comfortable, or go on a solo walk, then put a 20-minute timer on your phone and allow your mind to take you where it wants to take you. At first, it will probably take the opportunity to process some personal thoughts and feelings you haven't processed, and these are full of gems for your genius to develop too. But you might also find yourself wandering into great philosophical questions, energies, theories, and unseen realms. Each person with this gift will have a different place they dive deep into – you don't need to figure yours out so much as let your mind roam and follow it with enchantment.

Gift 34
Coming Alive

People with Gift 34 love that feeling of achieving things and feel best about themselves when they do.

The beauty of this gift is that when you show up in your power to anything, you inject a real force into that project or relationship or group that moves things forward. You're like the secret sauce for taking things over the finish line; and all you have to do is engage in things that Light you up, because those are the ones that will give you that fire that you can then spread to everyone else involved.

This is a very individual gift, meaning that when you focus on yourself and your achievements, actually everybody wins. It's energetically correct for you to be a bit selfish and focus on yourself and what you want to work toward.

When you do, there is a real power and force to the way you move through the world, and this not only teaches others the importance of being a bit selfish, sometimes in a good way, but also that power and force gives movement to the group projects you put your energy into.

The Deeper Level of This Gift

When you are doing things that Light you up, you activate your charismatic nature. You become bubbly and sparkly and effervescent, and this is the force that can move mountains. It draws other people into you, it gives a situation the spice that it needs to make it come alive. So many of us are doing and living and creating from a blasé, non-passionate place. Not you.

Essentially, when you come alive, everything and everyone you touch comes to life more too.

How to Flex This Gift

Allow yourself to show your fire, your excitement. Allow yourself to shine and be the subject of outside attention. It is not right for you to be shy or shrink to fit in. When you let yourself be in your full charisma, you actually make it easier for other people to rise too. Can you see how empowering this is? And to think that you almost wouldn't do it because the world has told you it's bad. We're afraid of shining our true magnificence that was given to us by the Divine – but consider how much better the world functions when we all do it. And consider you're one of the ones who's gonna pave the way for us: that's what you're here to do.

What Blocks This Gift

The world will tell you not to be so focused on yourself; do it anyway. The world will tell you it's selfish; but only once you do it will you see how that benefits so many others around you. Dare to give in to your go-getter nature and watch the rest flourish.

Gift 35
Sharing Your Experiences

Gift 35 is always looking for new things to experience; and once they've lived through something interesting, they love to share and pass it on with others. This is how we speed up our forward progression as a collective – pooling the findings and experiences each one of us gathers and turning it into gold. Gift 35 is someone that other people will love to live and learn vicariously through.

These people are the opposite of stagnant, because they like to keep things new and varied.

This keeps life fresh and interesting for themselves and others around them, ensuring Life stays colorful and that we get out of the familiar a bit. They are adept at pulling us toward trying new things that could better our lives, because most of us are hesitant and resist change.

Gift 35 does not hold on to things that don't serve it for very long, in any form, be that little things, like clothing, and bigger things, like jobs. If they're not enjoying it, it's out. They move quickly.

The best use of this gift is to pass on things you feel a genuine passion for *without* questioning its usefulness or validity – you just never know how it will become valuable, nor are you meant to. And don't talk about things just to get validation, worth, or belonging for others, because this compromises the integrity of your gift. Your voice is precious; reserving it for only times and topics that are truly Aligned will make the words you do speak go so much further.

How to Flex This Gift

Learn before you move on

Ideally, moving on to new things makes you wiser because you amass wisdom about yourself and life in doing so. Make sure that you're not just cycling through things for the novelty of them and then tossing them; reflect and get the wisdom from your previous thing before you move on completely to the next.

Good questions to ask are: 'What did that thing tell me about myself/life?' and 'What would be a more ideal way for things to be going forward?'

Get clear on what things you value and want to hold on to

Throughout your pursuit of new and novel things, there will be some that you want to keep for the longer term. However these might get boring to you after the novelty wears off, and you may end up not valuing them or taking them for granted. Find ways to bring newness to them and to keep things interesting – when you can do this you have truly mastered your gift.

And don't be afraid to let go of things that don't make you happy, but that society tells you you *have to* hold on to. Just because you've been told long relationships are good or that living in a home for 20 years is stable, that doesn't mean it's right for you.

Essentially, mastering this gift is bringing freshness and excitement to the things in your life you already love and discarding all the things that don't so you can find even more things you love. Don't ever be afraid to update and renew – *anything*.

What Blocks This Gift

Looking to the future at the expense of appreciating the present moment

Make sure you're not just being restless and never satisfied – take in all the good stuff you have manifested in your life as it's happening.

Impatience

Gift 35 gets bored when it seems like 'nothing is happening.' See those moments as the in-betweens, the breathers Life is giving you so you can do some reflecting before the next new thing comes in. When you can see life as a cycle of experiencing something and then reflecting, both of which are equally valuable, every moment of your life can start to feel like it's full of good stuff for you.

Gift 36
Turning Darkness into Light

The Surface Level of This Gift

Gift 36 are people who can really *feel* life deeply. Most of humanity puts all their attention on the daily to-and-fros, where Gift 36 sees the whole game: they effortlessly go under the hood and tap into the deeper layers of Life. And they *know* it's a fragile, heart-exploding, and heart-breaking miracle all at the same time. The depths to which they can feel what Life really is can both Light them up to the core and pierce them in the heart.

Because they're unusual in this way, they may mistake this ability for just being a bit crazy, silly, dramatic, or think they have to 'toughen up' a bit to be successful. In reality it is so evolved and wise to be this way: to see and go where other people can't or won't go. They are people brave enough to look at the shadows, drag them into the Light, only to see that, hey, they're not so bad or so scary after all. Maybe discomforts, fears, anxieties are just Light in disguise that the Universe *also* uses to help us evolve. Maybe they are blessings or have messages. Maybe they're beautiful parts of humanity too.

Learning to dance with the shadows and integrate them is how we transform into more Light. This is when Life becomes even sweeter and more joyful than our brains can dream up. With Gift 36, you can become a master in the realm of human feelings. And what is Life if not, for all the states it creates in our insides, a spectrum that unites us all no matter who we are.

The more Gift 36 people allow themselves to feel it all fully, the more their hearts open, and the more powerful they become. And in fully embracing their connection with Life, they model what kind of life is possible for others too.

On a Deeper Level

These are people who can really understand all people. Because they have this ability to feel super deep, they can feel how someone else is feeling, even if they themselves haven't gone through the exact same situation or hardship. This is a gift of deep empathy and compassion. But more than that, they are meant to use this deep understanding of the human experience to better whatever it is that they offer and do with their life.

How to Flex This Gift

Remember your Light power

You are at your best when you are unafraid to look at the negative, while also remembering that the negative is never more powerful than you. Never bigger than your ability to conquer it or transmute it. Never so threatening or shameful or overwhelming that you can't overcome it. The more you cultivate faith in your own capabilities, faith in the goodness of the Universe, and faith in how everything that comes our way is perfect for us, the more you'll float over the darkness and slay it – with Grace. And not necessarily because you have to fight and suppress it head on – but because you are unafraid enough to lovingly shine a light on it, while remaining unattached to it, which is all that's needed for it to dissolve.

Don't be afraid or judgmental of your darkness

For you, there is so much wisdom in it, and you're meant to go there, mine for the gold, and use that gold to lift your world up. Let there be no emotion, no fear, no negative situation so 'bad' that you can't look at it and get clear on exactly what's going on here. Because what you find when you look IS the very magic the Universe wants to implant in you by way of sending you that so-called bad situation in the first place.

And then, no matter what you create from that magic, whether you speak or write about it, create a product out of it, or spread that gold at your workplace, this is true Alchemy – transmuting the dark into Light.

What Blocks This Gift

Taking the darkness so heavily

Darkness is not personal; we all have it. Seeing its universality will help you feel how whole you are, how whole you've always been, and in turn how everybody else is too. Emotions are simply transient visitors, here to help us and enhance our experience.

Similarly it's important you don't seek out the lows because of the drama. Just because you CAN feel lows, it doesn't mean there's any validity in seeking them out for the sake of it or making them become your identity. They can leave just as quickly as they arrive, especially when we don't take them so heavily or feel afraid of them. When you feel into the depths *while* keeping your own state as bright and high as possible, that's the magic formula that snuffs *out* darkness. We can't change the darkness into anything if we're loving staying in dramatic states ourselves.

Once you've got to this place of keeping faith and hope no matter what you look at, you can help others realize there are no depths they can't transform either.

Gift 37
Fostering Togetherness

At the Surface Level

Family time and togetherness is everything to those with Gift 37; whether that's their actual family or friends that are family, Gift 37 is the one keeping everybody together.

Gift 37 is happiest at a dinner table, surrounded by their people. This kind of togetherness is what sustains community and closeness, and it's a very undervalued gift in the world today. But think about it; we've never been so disconnected, and so much of what we long for is to commune. You have a very, very valuable skill, and you'll see it become even more valuable in the coming years.

At the Deeper Level

You are here to model true togetherness, which is not based on who's higher and who's lower, who's cool and who's not, but warmth and openness to everyone. For those with Gift 37 – this is your time! Society today is so fractured and separated, and you are here to glue it back together with this consciousness of inclusiveness. Live it, breathe it, model it in your own life and in the way you show up in the world.

You can apply this gift on a movie set, at a drinks party, in the office. You can be a party planner, a yoga studio owner, a personal assistant. As long as bringing people together is a facet of what you bring to the table, you're doing it right.

How to Flex This Gift

Get rid of any sense of hierarchy in your own mind

We are taught to assess people when we meet them and to place them as either above or below us: stronger, weaker, more powerful, less powerful. But this is the consciousness of separation, and this blocks your Inclusiveness. There can only be unconditional love, which is your gift, when there is no hierarchy left. Start by dissolving it in your own way of seeing life, by asking yourself who you put yourself above and below.

Be inclusive to your Self

The more loving and open-hearted you are with yourself – a.k.a. there is togetherness between all parts of you, the more others will see you as having this gift too.

What Blocks This Gift

Codependence

Bring people together from an excited, giving place, because you're sharing from your heart, not because you feel responsible for making everyone happy. Not because the value of your giving is dependent on how well it's received. Some people won't value communing as much as you do; that's not to say they're wrong or that you are, it's just that they're on a different path to you and prioritize differently. Do it for people who really enjoy it too. That's when the gift will multiply like crazy (and when you'll feel the most fulfilled too).

Gift 38
Taking a Stand

Gift 38 is a very primal gift. This is the matriarchal or patriarchal protectress/protector that isn't afraid to go into battle for love.

Those who possess it love a fight, because they know that on the other side of it, when done with the right consciousness, they can reach or create a better situation than the one in front of them right now. They're not discouraged by problems or obstacles, and they have the willingness to cut through them.

They are stubborn, persistent, love to get their hands dirty, and feel alive when they're fighting – and that's all a good thing. These things are all here to support you living your highest Purpose, and they're pointing you toward living the life of a warrior, where you're the one among us who doesn't give up the road to a better life, better way, better relationships, just because there is some s*** that needs to be addressed or overcome in order to make it happen.

The only thing that determines whether a gift is negative or positive is the consciousness with which we use it. We need people who are unafraid to back down when tensions arise. We need people who are here to fight the good fight. This is what you're here for, Gift 38.

How to Flex This Gift

Fight with an open heart

We've been taught to fight with a me-versus-you mentality. But you are here to pioneer fighting with togetherness and love. You can call people out lovingly. You can point out what people did wrong with understanding and compassion. When they close up or get defensive, you can stay at a high vibration of lovingly engaging. This is not only the route of creating better outcomes after a fight, but of also modeling the kind of conflict that people feel safer doing.

Figure out what you stand for

If you don't feel like you're fighting a good fight and helping the world (whether that's your world or the wider world) become better, you feel purposeless and restless. You can even lose your passion and enthusiasm for life. Look around at what makes you mad or impassioned, what you feel is unjust or simply 'could be better' – those are exactly the areas you're meant to head right into and get involved in.

What Blocks This Gift

Keeping it in

Because you need to be taking a stand to feel alive, if you haven't found your causes and your mission, you could unconsciously be picking fights or taking things out on people without knowing it. This gift is wanting to come out, and it would rather come out *somewhere* than not at all. Similarly, if you try to bottle it up because you only have negative associations with being a fighter, you will be tired all the time or create pent-up tension or aggression. The more you funnel this incredible gift toward things that really matter to you, the more at peace in yourself you will be.

Gift 39
Rousing Spirit

On the Surface Level

Gift 39 is here to shake things up. You have been given this naturally provocative, playful, and even flirtatious energy because you're here to jolt people awake a bit, and to do this, you have to make an impact.

On a Deeper Level

You are here to bring emotion out of others so that they can feel more in touch with their Spirit. Most of us are on automatic, half-asleep mode through most of our days, and yet we all want to feel more alive and connected to our inner Self. You are here to bring us closer to that.

Because of this, it's *good* for you to rock the boat, to rouse people a little, or try to get a reaction out of them. The intention you put behind it is your biggest work. When you do it for things that will help connect people to their human, emotional, Spirit side, you're living your Divine Purpose. Think about the times people feel most alive – it's when their inner Spirit is roused. Whether that's from a movie that really stirred something in them, from a passionate conversation with a loved one, or a situation that came along and really made them pay attention, it doesn't matter.

When you are unafraid to spark people awake, whatever avenues and passions you put your energy into will have the ability to move people to the core in this way.

How to Flex This Gift

Let go of people's initial reactions to you

Whether they have a good or bad reaction to it at the beginning doesn't really matter. What matters is: Have you woken them up out of their daze and roused emotions that were stirring under their surface? If so, you have elevated them, no matter whether they felt happy about it initially or not. Making their Spirit stir sets off a chain of inner journeying and feeling that can lead them to becoming more alive, more self-aware, and more 'on purpose.'

Embrace wanting attention

You are made to seek attention because that's the Universe's way of making sure your provocation gets noticed. Attention is only a bad thing to want if it's coming from a negative place. If it's because you know it's necessary for you to fulfill your mission, it's Divine and totally Aligned.

What Blocks This Gift

Suppressing your own emotions

If you are afraid to express the fullness of your own emotions, you dull your ability to spark it in others. You would only do this because society teaches us it's more grown up and together to be more emotionless. But you are here to help us come back to remembering that it's feeling, not thinking, that helps us get to know who we are.

Rousing people when you yourself are reactive

Anger is a temporary state that happens when you feel you have been wronged. It's what we call an initial feeling, rather than a true feeling, and if you follow it, it will guide you toward a deeper feeling(s), such as fear, sadness, or apathy; when you provoke from a place of anger, you haven't got to your true emotions yet, and so any provocation created from that space won't elevate others either. Work through your initial reactions in private, turn them into self-knowledge and becoming more whole in yourself. And *then* go out into the world and make your magic.

Gift 40
The Giver

Gift 40 loves to give to their circle of people, and that's one of their primary motivations in life. You are designed to want to work hard and generously share the rewards you receive in return for this hard work.

You are here to become a breadwinner, the patriarch of your own life. Not in the way that you have to out-earn everybody, but that you generously share the fruits of your labor with those you care about. Gift 40 is a very nurturing and magnanimous energy, whereby you thrive and shine, and everybody benefits.

How to Flex This Gift

Do the kind of 'hard work' that's fun to you

When you make sure your hard work is enjoyable and is something you're good at, it won't deplete you in the process. After all, you're meant to give to yourself just as much as you give to others. When you find work that is right for you, it will energize you and feed you rather than exhaust you – and this will allow your star to rise even more, and shine on so many more people.

Sometimes the difference between energizing and exhausting work is the job itself, and sometimes it's your mental approach to it. Both can be fixed, you just have to get clear on which one it is.

Accept and ask for support yourself

Because you so voluntarily support others, the thing you value receiving from others most is also support.

This is usually in the form of recognition, and that's a healthy thing. People with this gift are motivated by being seen and praised – whether that's on a small scale, just by their family, or on a larger scale, like being famous or lauded.

The problem is that Gift 40 is often uncomfortable with asking for support, recognition, and gratitude. And there may be tons of people around you who *do* appreciate you tremendously, but don't feel like you *need* support because, most likely, you act like you have it all together. Don't be afraid to show your humanness too.

What Blocks This Gift

Over-giving

You can get to a point where you're over-giving so much that no amount of support and appreciation can fill that deficit. With everything we do in life, there has to be a balance of giving and receiving, and by over-giving you are preventing that balance, ensuring that it will blow up in the future in some way, because a person on either end will feel guilt or resentment, harbor negative feelings, etc. Give from your Soul, and only to the amount that feels good to you, and don't give in to your ego that will convince you that giving more will always make you a better person.

Gift 41
Seeing Future Possibilities

These people have a special skill of seeing future possibilities – their brains are like supercomputers that can see every possible outcome from a situation. When something arises, they can effortlessly see all of the potential scenarios in about two split seconds. This ability is like an instant download, so you 'see' things before you've even had time to make sense of them.

They are often seen to have wild imaginations or big visions, which isn't really wild at all – it comes from the fact that they can see the full scope of what the near future could be. Most of us have a much more limited scope in what we see 'could' happen. You see *all* the things that could happen.

On a deeper level, they're connected to the energy field where all creative expression exists, and they are here to bring outside-the-box things into the physical world. In this field, all possible outcomes from any situation exist – which gives them the ability to see every possible way something could unfold – in their own lives and in the wider world. They are cause-and-effect masters.

Whenever you feel unconnected to your creative thinking, a repetitive activity that triggers your brain into motion will always bring you back – this could be doodling, making notes, cooking, writing. It doesn't have to be super artistic and professional, although it can be. It just has to be something that helps you singularly focus and slow your thoughts.

They are also impulsive and always yearning for that something new that will make them feel more alive, though sometimes they don't know what that thing is. They often have an itch and can live for this certain thing they believe is gonna change their whole life when it happens, which can make them restless, even if it's just a low-level, background kind of restless.

How to Flex This Gift

Act on what you see

This gift is a guidance from the Universe showing you what to do next. If you can conceive of some new creative offering, that's a sign that you're meant to be the one that creates it. If you can see an outcome that no one else can see, hold strong to it and know that it's possible. Shoot for it. If you see a potential, and you don't strive to make it real, you will get caught up too much in the world of ideas, which will cause excessive worry and thinking without achieving to the same heights you desire.

Have patience and understanding for people who don't 'see' the vision the way you do

There would be no use in everyone having the same skills. Inevitably, there will be a lag between you seeing something and others seeing it – which can be frustrating, I know. But you have to fight that at every turn. Just know that you don't have to force them to get it, you just have to have such strong faith in the unseen before it's made manifest. That certainty is what will get others to see it the quickest too.

What Blocks This Gift

Strike the balance between living in the world of potentials and living in the now

Don't let your ability to see all potentials draw you away from appreciating what is in front of you today. They can get stuck in always feeling like something's incomplete because they know there is always more to be brought into the world. But don't mistake that as your current life not being satisfying enough. Don't let it rob you of seeing the joy that's right in front of you.

Don't let the fact that there is always more make you feel like you're in lack

When this gift is used incorrectly, you will feel like someone else's life is always better than yours. You can have chronic thoughts of,

'They've got it better than I have,' or 'My life would be so much better if I did/experienced this.' The more thoughts you have like this, the more you will drain your own ability to manifest your great potential. Don't let those illusions pull you off your path. There is always more for everybody, and your duty is to bring in whatever's meant for you.

Gift 42
Realizing Potential

Gift 42 is here to make sure that growth happens. It wants to ensure that the maximum potential is made real/manifested out of every person and every situation.

This shows up as a strong desire in you to create and expand and have things work out in the best way possible. To accomplish great things.

It's easy for you to have positive, abundant outlooks, and this lends itself to you creating success for yourself and others.

With this big desire comes a heightened awareness of everything that stands in the way of the greatness unfolding, which is another skill you can lend to so many different projects and areas of life. You are very good at overcoming blockages and helping others see their blockages, because your mind sees them so clearly. Even when things get hard, you can self-examine and see how you're getting in your own way. This gift gets stronger the more you allow yourself to get quiet and observe.

There is a caveat with this gift, like all other gifts, that it won't bear fruit if you use it only on yourself. If you are solely focused on realizing your own potential, the whole thing will short-circuit. You have to take an interest in using your skills to ensure other people's potential where you can, too, and it's written in your stars that when you do this, abundance will flow to you. Truly, genuinely wanting others to succeed is the secret ingredient that makes the whole cake rise.

How to Flex This Gift

Getting clear on the specific ways you're good at helping people make their potential real

This isn't about going overboard, doing anything and everything to lift other people up, this is about figuring out where and how you're good at helping people live out their potential and making that a big part of what you offer to the world. The more you can laser in on where *you* add value, the more value you'll be able to bring.

What Blocks This Gift

Sacrificing your own goals to help others rise

There has to be a healthy balance here. You can't just be helping others match up to their potential at your detriment. If you're doing it for work, charge market price for it. If you're a full-time mom and wife, don't deplete yourself trying to make sure that everyone rises but yourself. You get the picture.

Let go of trying to create a specific outcome too tightly – and remember that if you put good consciousness and Aligned energy behind it, the best outcome will happen. Sometimes, that outcome is one you can't even imagine yet, but it will materialize if you show up your best way possible.

A focus on getting results can sometimes mean you're more comfortable with the ending and not so much in the process. What you have to remember, though, is that life is always a cycle of new beginnings, the process, and then the ending, and after that ending, something will start all over again. 'Endings' may feel good, but they are an illusion. Don't mistake manifesting potential for what looks like nice little conclusions and endings on a shallow level – focus more on living out our potential in this long game called life.

Don't rush to get to the end so much that you miss the lessons, because if that's the case, you will go through a new cycle, sure, but the same patterns and themes will come up until you have integrated them in yourself.

Gift 43
Epiphanies

People with this gift often get flashes of brilliance where they see things in a way that's miles ahead of its time. These insights probably don't even feel that special to you, it's just 'how you see things,' your natural point of view. But make no mistake, you think in a futuristic way.

You came here to share the way you see things with others, to leap us forward into the future. There are better ways of doing things and seeing things that can upgrade the way we do life, and you are a specialist at this in at least one area, but usually, over the course of your life, this will extend/spread far and wide to apply to many specialties.

You are here to jolt us forward – not gradually, but by taking quantum leaps in understanding. So don't ever dull or soften your vision of the future to make it more palatable to others, because that takes away the power of the effect.

Although this gift sounds lofty, it's rooted in efficiency and making our lives easier and better. So it can run the gamut from glamorous upgrades, to more everyday ones, for example, like stationary: think of how many people get more productive and creative when they have a perfect office setup with all the little office supplies and systems that make everything easy and streamlined.

How to Flex This Gift

Share these insights in the right time, to the right people

Start taking note (either literally or mentally) about the unusual ways you see life. People with genius often take it for granted and don't even see how unique and valuable it is. The more you become crystal clear on where and how you see things differently, the easier it will be to share it with others – and you'll know the right people who need it and the right situations to speak up in. And when you are in this constant state of contributing to others like this, what you say will be communicated beautifully.

On the other hand, if you hold these insights in for fear of others not recognizing your genius, or because *you* don't value that genius, or out of just not sharing consistently enough, it will bubble up inside you and sometimes cause you to blurt things out that will come out either super bluntly or incoherently. People won't 'get' your genius when it comes out this way, which will only cement your belief that others don't value you.

Value your wisdom the exact same as you value others' wisdom, even though it looks different.

Strike the balance of honoring your own genius enough, versus also taking in and valuing the insights of others. Usually people with this gift will veer too far in one of these directions, and as a result, they feel like they're always drowning in their own thoughts or worries.

What Blocks This Gift

Worrying that people won't understand you

When you hold the belief that others won't 'get' you, it's a self-fulfilling prophecy because it either makes you over explain, hold back, judge, or get annoyed and frustrated as you do speak – all of which make others not as interested in what you're saying. Say things the way they make sense to you and trust that that will be like a homing signal, drawing all those who are destined recipients of your words to you. And at the perfect timing no less.

Getting frustrated that others seem far behind

Again, the reason you're here at this very time is because there are people who will understand you *and* adore the quantum leaps, upgrades, and efficiencies you bring to them. There wouldn't be much use if everyone else could do this too – it's a diverse range of skills we possess collectively that makes our world so likely to rise.

Gift 44
Spotting Patterns and Turning Them into Wisdom

With Gift 44, you're a whizz at spotting patterns and trends and being able to predict what's coming next.

You can look at all the things that have been so far and see the obvious next progression. Their minds automatically go – 'if *a* and *b* have been before, then *c* will follow.'

This gift will show up in the areas of life they're interested in, whether that's fashion, tech, sciences, or general life.

This effortless ability to see patterning also applies to people: you instinctively know who is Aligned with who. You can sniff out which people are a good fit for each other – in work, relationships, and friendships. Like with every gift, you can also spot this for your own life.

In every pattern, there is wisdom and intel. You are here to use this wisdom to improve the way we do things, to put people together in a better way, and to predict what's coming next.

A knack for patterning means you will tell how things are going to evolve: whose relationships will go well and what events will likely follow on from the current situation.

In your own life, if you have this gift, you came here to really learn from your history and use that as guidance on how to show up differently today. This makes you an expert at evolution; the trick is to use the past to create a better vision of the future and not the same vision as what's already been.

How to Flex This Gift

This gift has to be practiced

Like all intuitive gifts, the more you take note of them, the louder the messages become. How good you are at this gift is in direct proportion to how much you listen out for it, trust it, and then act accordingly.

When you don't listen, it's like saying you're not interested in that Intuition, so Life doesn't send as much of it your way.

A good way to start a relationship with this gift is writing down (whether on paper or just on your phone) all the little things it says to you, even if you're not quite ready to act on them yet. Just being truthful about what the messages are, with yourself, is already a giant step in the right direction – especially when the messages are kind of inconvenient. You acknowledging them anyway is a serious power move.

What Blocks This Gift

Not believing any 'off' feelings you get about people or situations just because you can't explain why

Part of what you're here to learn with this gift is that things don't always have to 'make sense' on paper to be true. Instinct is the oldest form of intelligence – trust it.

Fear of the past repeating itself

You can (consciously or unconsciously) be ruled by an assumption that whatever bad experiences happened to you before, will happen again. The logic is – the past predicts the future. But here's the thing: just because you can *sometimes* see trends and causalities in life, it doesn't mean that there is *only* that. Life is also full of random, spontaneous events, and sharp pivots. Remind yourself that people's lives also change overnight, that the future is a totally blank canvas that you can create whatever you want on it, and that negative experiences only have a hold on your life if you choose to carry them with you.

Gift 45
Resourceful Solutions

Gift 45 lives in the real world and knows how to make the most of a situation to maximize the wealth, well-being, and happiness of the people involved. Gift 45 looks at what you've got and can tell you how to *work* with what you've got.

Making money is one thing. Gift 45 is adept at keeping it, saving it, stretching it, and the best ways to use it once you've got it.

The same is true with how we rule our affairs as a family or a team; Gift 45 knows which of us are best at which roles, who's meant to do what for the benefit of everybody.

In your physical well-being, too, Gift 45 can meet you right where you're at, wherever you need help, and knows what practical steps will help you improve.

When you're in dire straits, Gift 45 will know how to get you back to safety, and when you're just okay, Gift 45 can tell you how to make it a little better.

How to Flex This Gift

Help with a loving heart

This gift is strongly rooted in ensuring security and survival for people. So it is practical, but we often assume that means you have to be harsh or detached, where actually those things are unrelated. Remember that you can be kick-ass levels of practical AND loving and warm at the same time. Stay connected to the compassion you have for people as you do it. This gift will shine the most when you do.

What Blocks This Gift

Focusing on what you don't have

If you focus on what's missing, you'll block your ability to work with what you *do* have. The best asset for a person with Gift 45 is the attitude that not only is the glass half-full, but that they can always see the action steps to turn that half into a full.

Don't confuse challenges with problems

Because you shine at making the best out of things, you're often looking at less than ideal scenarios. Don't ever let that make you feel that life is full of problems, or make you feel frustrated that things are never good, or that things could be more perfect. They *can* be more perfect, but that's life's journey, and we have to find a way to show up for that with excitement and hope. *We* are the ones who create ideals and happiness every time we infuse it into everything we do, and when we put our gifts to good use in the world. Challenges are here so that we can create something better, always.

Gift 46
Embodiment

One of the things you came here to do in this lifetime is learn to love your physical body. For you, celebrating your physical experience is crucial – your body is an instrument that you need to put to use in sharing your gifts with the world. You aren't the type who can just sit behind a computer; you need to be using and moving your physicality.

Nurturing and celebrating your body, with exercise, self-care rituals, and a good diet is also a key component in what you came to embody on this Earth.

If you have a tendency to live in the mind, this gift is showing you that your dreams will unfold with so much more ease and lightness when you learn to let go of thoughts and analysis and prioritize your feelings and five senses more. The body makes things simple, the mind complicates.

This gift is about loving your body, but really, it's about finding Lightness. Our minds make things heavy by holding on to things and overthinking, whereas the body just wants to be present and relish the physical experience, which is such a lighter way to live. This is what you came here to nail down and then be that example for others. We all want to feel more free and at ease – this is how we get there.

Let go of the past, let go of your stories, and be that person who is tickled and delighted by the magic of everyday life – because that's what Gift 46 people really are.

Ultimately, you just have to keep remembering that what makes Life 'life,' is the fact that we have physical bodies on an earthly plane. It's through the gateway of the body that everything actually takes place.

When you start using your body as a portal to all you want to create with this Life, you'll start to enjoy new levels of mind-body connection, where the body can give you clues into your thoughts, beliefs, and emotions, and where by changing any of those things, you can see your physical experience become noticeably better.

The body is such an overlooked tool; you are here to model its magic.

How to Flex This Gift

Trust that the body knows better than the mind

You've been taught that you have to be constantly on top of everything and in control for things to happen the way you want them to be: nothing could be further from the truth. With this gift, you have a natural ability to find yourself in the right place at the right time, but you're probably not even seeing it because overthinking puts blinders on you and prevents you from seeing the opportunities that lay right in front of you. When you clear your mind and go with what your body wants, you will receive so much more guidance and clear direction.

What Blocks This Gift

Body struggles

Even though the wisdom of this gift is that our bodies are our biggest blessings, the world will teach you the opposite: that we have to control them, that they're a burden, that we have to be at odds with them. We can't trust their desires, for food, rest, sensuality, or sex. Often, this is the journey with Gift 46 – un-learning all this messaging and making friends with your body again.

Being at odds or disconnected with your body can show up as: overeating, undereating, numbing with any substances, being overly or under-sexual, shaming your natural desires, and thus preferring to pretend you don't have them.

Your connection with your body is one of your biggest power secrets. Try being on the same side as your body, treating it like your best friend, and watch how much more peace and ease your wishes unfold with. You won't even feel like you're 'doing' anything.

Gift 47
Reinvention

All that is wrong with your life, and life in general, *really* gets you down, Gift 47. You have this deep fear of 'What if it all amounts to nothing?' This is for a *good* reason – to ensure that it *does* amount to its greatest potential! You are skilled at seeing the distance between where things are now and how much greater they could be, and this causes you just enough discomfort or pain to make you totally unafraid to break past all the holding patterns that keep us stuck in our comfort zones. You are here to constantly transform and to help others do the same.

You have a strong connection to your greatest version of yourself, and it's like you feel constantly pulled toward becoming her/him. You are keenly aware of your destiny and want to fulfill it more than anything.

Because of this, you're not afraid to let go of anything about yourself that might stand in the way of that.

When you really lean in to this gift, it's about being unafraid to shed any parts of your identity so you can become something greater.

This makes you a pro at transformation, because there is nothing about your identity that you would keep if it prevents you from fulfilling what you want. You know you're really living this gift right when you're changing little, sometimes seemingly irrelevant, things about you all the time.

How to Flex This Gift

Embrace abstract thinking

Your brain is not linear, it's abstract – you don't get answers by trying to problem solve the way the world has taught you. Whenever you try to think in linear, analytical ways when it comes to creating change, you're going against your nature.

For you, think less about how to fix the present and dream more about what the better way looks like – and then do that. Don't resolve the old, conceive the new. Implement new micro little ways of being, from habits, ways of thinking, your posture, anything that reflects a more powerful embodied version of you – and they will create big shifts in your energetic blueprint.

Relax

Whenever you feel pressured to find a solution in life, it won't come, whereas when you relax and tune in to the overall feeling or energy of the situation, everything will come flooding in. You invite your natural way of thinking in, which is based more on having spontaneous revelations and conceptions.

What Blocks This Gift

Overanalyzing the past and trying to fit it in to nice, neat little narratives

There is this pressure inside you that will try to make sense out of your past to make it all count for something. Not everything needs to make sense. Sometimes you can just let things be. And anyway, looking at the past only helps to the extent that it inspires the new. Don't get stuck in it.

Needing to make sense of other people's life story

Resist the need to make sense of things by relating it to your own experience; remember that not everything fits into your personal frame/viewpoint, and we can never truly understand someone else's journey. If you spend too much of this gift trying to do that, you will get stuck in comparison and judgment and, not to mention, drain your energy away from the more positive aspect: reinvention.

Gift 48
A Well of Wisdom

You are a very deep human being if you have Gift 48.

You have a huge internal life, where you feel things so deeply, and you can tap into what's beneath the surface so easily. This is one of those gifts where it's easy to assume everyone is like this, but they're really not. You haven't had to 'work' for this gift, and you probably don't even see how much of a gift it is yet – though it really is.

Because of this ability to tap in deep, you naturally possess true wisdom, an intuitive understanding of how life's cogs work.

This wisdom is a deep well, a limitless resource that others can come to whenever they need to develop their own wisdom.

One of the reasons you don't see the full scope of this gift, is that wisdom and depth only comes out in the moment, when there's a need for it. Once something actually happens in real time, that's when the clarity drops in. Or when someone else has a conundrum, you catch yourself knowing what it's all about. It's in those moments you can see what a highly developed EQ you have. But most of the time, you're highly unaware of this gift, and you can be plagued by this false belief that you don't 'have what it takes,' that you are incompetent and couldn't possibly accomplish what you desire to.

How to Flex This Gift

Prioritize your emotional development

Doing inner work and being in touch with your feelings and intuitions is a super important component to you achieving your Purpose – it's like your secret weapon, because those feelings are intel, which always contain guidance on how to turn something into something better.

Face your fears

In the depths of every human being lies our greatest magic and our greatest darkness. They are locked in there together. The more we are okay to look at what our fears are, the more magic reveals itself. Especially for you, Gift 48 – the deeper you go, the more fulfilled you will be. Don't apologize or hide your depth simply because the world has taught you that emotional depth is counter to intelligence, as this will always keep you out of your kind of intelligence – innate life wisdom.

How to Unblock This Gift

Don't let your mind convince you something is missing in you

When you have such a vast inner landscape, you see the gaps and lacks so much more clearly. You also have no visibility on what you're capable of until you put it into motion. So ironically, being so deep can make you feel like you don't have what it takes. It's as if there are certain things other people possess that make them successful, happy, etc. that you don't have, which leads you to fear that you'll never get there yourself. If you look back at your life, you'll see that you always got the answers at exactly the right times they were needed – this is Gift 48 at work. And the more you can really see how this has always happened, the more you will trust that you will actually always receive 'what it takes' on your journey to set you up to succeed every step of the way.

Gift 49
The Humanitarian

With this gift, you have a deep yearning to change the world, and probably have since childhood even if you didn't know how. You are here to be a revolutionary, because that's a big archetype that makes you who you are.

True revolutionaries and change makers aren't the ones who ruffle feathers for the sake of it or criticize from the soap box. In fact, there is so much ego that creates that kind of obvious revolt.

You're here to help bring about the kinds of changes that make people approach life with more compassion, softness and openness, to dissolve judgment, to make us work as one.

You are best when you approach it as – we only succeed when everybody wins. So being part of movements, products, services that provide a win-win is a huge signpost for you. For example, a power source alternative that benefits the consumer AND the planet, an initiative that helps the underprivileged (which also allows generous people with a great option of where to give money to), something that makes people's lives more aesthetically pleasing but also makes them think or is ethical. You get the picture.

Change through innovation and inventiveness is a quiet revolution, but a revolution nonetheless. However, you *could* also genuinely be someone who is meant to be the kind of revolutionary that speaks truth, expresses anger, and rouses the masses – you'll know depending on the rest of your chart (and also because you'll feel it in your heart). Just make sure you do it with love and with the intention of uniting people instead of judging those who still have a ways to go in their evolution of consciousness.

A good way to ask if you're on the right track with whatever change making you're participating in is to ask yourself the question: 'Is this helping people evolve internally too?' That could be mental, physical, spiritual, or emotional, but as long as you're offering the potential for growth and improvement, you're good.

How to Flex This Gift

Don't be afraid to look at what you think is wrong with the world and with us as a society. You can only create what's so right when you fearlessly get crystal clear on what *you* see is wrong. Every person with this gift will see different things and understand that whichever ones are coming to you are the ones the Universe wants *you* to focus your attention on.

The ruse is though: you have to include your own self and consciousness in looking for what's wrong. Be open to noticing where you still judge others, where your separation mindset gets in the way, and, very pertinent for those with Gift 49 – where you pull away and distance yourself from others, especially when upset or angry. Use your own experience to inform you about what other humans are thinking and feeling, too, and when you tap in to how this thinking shows up in you, you can not only use it to inform and improve what you're contributing to the world, but also help you see truly how similar, and 'all in this together' we really are.

What Blocks This Gift

Fear of rejection

People with this gift want to create unity and harmony so much that they extra-fear being rejected. It's likely that you will read the tiniest, most subtle behaviors in other people as rejection of you when they're probably not. Just be aware of when you feel rejected or abandoned and, in those moments, attempt to zoom out and see the interaction through a more objective lens. Try your hardest also not to reject or leave situations out of a need to be the person that exits out first. Try to show up and be honest about how you're feeling, in a soft and open way, because this creates a revolutionary new dynamic between two people in a personal way, which is just as important a revolution to create as the ones you're gonna do on a wider level. In fact, it sets the stage for it.

Gift 50
A Strong Value System

You are born with a strong sense of right and wrong when it comes to human behavior.

You hold yourself to a high standard of integrity and moral conduct, and this is part of what you're here to do for others – to be an example and to create more fairness and honor when interacting with each other. This gift is so ingrained in you that it's like a strong inner knowing, and you find it difficult to do wrong, especially if you know it.

Whether you try to or not, you're a gatekeeper of morality, and others who know you already sense a strong moral compass and dedication to fairness, even if they can't put their finger on it.

Even though we tend to think of right and wrong as fixed things, they're actually fluid. Different societies, at different times in history, and different small groups within the wider society, all need different value systems that will serve their highest good the best. So this gift is not an intellectual, dogmatic gift based in the mind; it's actually based in Intuition, because it's about tuning into what values are serving people and which ones aren't, at any given time and in any given situation.

With this gift comes a natural diplomacy, because when you're in a group, you're like a gel that makes everyone else get on better together. Usually, you don't have to consciously 'do' anything to make this happen, it just happens when you add someone who has moral integrity into a group – your standards create a template that invites others to rise up to.

How to Flex This Gift

Keep evolving your own values

It's good to keep asking yourself what values that we still hold dear are actually out of date, maybe they were passed down to us from previous generations, but they're no longer relevant or of use. The more you become aware, update, and mold your own value system, and stay fluid and open, the more you'll find yourself in powerful positions in society where you'll have influence over justice for many. This is because, when you get your integrity absolutely on the money, Life will want to use you to have that gift make maximum impact.

So for example, you want to stay away from rigid thinking like 'this is *always* bad' or '*only* this is good.' The world will tempt you to think in absolutes because it creates a false sense of safety, but actually, to ensure the safety and success of all humans, we need to be much more flexible and assess on a case-by-case basis. Trust that your Intuition will always sniff out the outcomes, decisions, and conduct that will benefit everybody, in any situation you'll find yourself in. You don't need to pre-decide anything.

You can get preachy if you're called to, but without judgment

Remember that fairness and morality are not that obvious to others as they are to you – they're not 'not getting it', that's just not where their gifts lie.

What Blocks This Gift

Fear of responsibility, which is really the fear of being your Highest Self

With this ability to see right and wrong, you feel a huge (mostly unconscious) pressure to be an example and an authority, in yourself and also out in the world, and often that is your biggest fear – the responsibility that that brings. Life is calling you to own this gift, grab it by the reins, and run with it unapologetically. You were made to be an authority in this life – it's your duty to share it.

If you feel blocked to rise up, realize that being an authority doesn't put you higher than others, just that this is your specific mission.

Some questions to help you un-block might be: What do you associate responsibility with? Being judged or criticized, being separate or different from others, it weighing hard on your shoulders, that having power makes you 'bad'? Once you can put your finger on your specific fear around this and look at it for the irrational belief that it is, you can start to dissolve it and create more desire to feel the fear, but go ahead and step up regardless.

Gift 51
Shaker-Upper

Gift 51 gives you an ability to make an impact on people, whether you try to or not. You're a very daring individual human being who came here to color outside the lines – and help us all do the same.

Most of the time, what humans call 'life' is actually a very small frame that they have accepted and squeezed themselves into – physically, mentally, emotionally, and spiritually. And they won't be expanded out of that, much less busted out of that, unless someone shakes them up a little bit; that's you. It's the role of an enlightener. Maybe you do that by shocking them, maybe by being a little daring, direct, or controversial, or maybe just by waking people up to new truths – the right way to do this gift is the one that feels authentic to you. None of these are better or worse; if you do them with heart and compassion, you are being a Lightworker.

How to Flex This Gift

Make friends with your ambition

Your Soul chose to want to make an impact on people because following that is part of you becoming your Highest Self. So don't judge your desire to impact people as bad, or question whether you're worthy of impacting people. It's not about 'you' – the Universe has already allocated this gift to you, so you may as well accept that and do something beautiful with it. Impact is what will ensure that your Essence (through your words, contributions, and actions) reaches people the way it's meant to.

What Blocks This Gift

Negative associations you've been given with being impactful

People tend to judge, shame, or shut down this kind of big shaker-up quality – mostly because they're afraid of being shaken out of their *own* comfort zones. The thing with banality/'normalcy' is it's comfortable and knowable. So you fear your impactful side because other people fear it. But it's one of those fears where, as real as they'll feel to people, once they're introduced to a bigger box, it's like they forgot all about that fear altogether. You are a person who has this power to instantly uplevel people's boxes. But in order to do that, you have to embrace that side and trust when the Universe is prompting you to be in that gift.

Shed the stories you may have inherited that being this way makes you unintelligent or attention seeking. And remind yourself there's nothing inherently bad with wanting impact, wanting to be shocking, arousing, controversial – it depends on the intention you plug into it. The more you do it in the good way, the more the world will get to re-understand this quality for what it is.

Don't be shocking out of boredom or because you yourself just want to 'feel'

Do it when your heart is truly calling you to. Misuse of this gift is what will get the negative results that we normally associate with people who are shocking and impactful.

Gift 52
Sitting Still to Get Results

Your natural energy is calm and grounded. You are someone who gets so much clarity in stillness. You tend to stay in one place and not move around so much, which is a *good* thing for you – you're not meant to be rushing around like the rest of the world.

When you lean into your stillness, there is a timeless, immovable quality to you that is extremely attractive to other people. You are classic, stable, unfazed – which is such a relief and a welcome resting place for us in today's world.

You don't get swept up in the moment, caught up in current crazes, or get phased by chaos. You have a vantage point that knows not to get sucked into any of these temporary things, and as a result, you have a wisdom that sees the much bigger picture. Embrace that you are more 'still' than other people and see that as a power.

If you try to run around like a headless chicken and create a whir of activity like you see others doing, you will lose this gift of clarity and wisdom. If you complicate and overfill your life, you won't have that simplicity that allows you to see Truth. And not only will that make you feel unsure in your own life, but also you won't be able to guide others with the wisdom that stillness gives you.

How to Flex This Gift

Only move when you feel moved to

The world will make you feel like you have to 'get up and do' every day. But you have to stop trying to achieve this way and do it your unique way: if you stay still and peaceful, you'll start to notice energy build up inside you, urging or nudging you toward something. When you allow it time to build up enough, it'll become such a strong urge that you can't *help* but do something about it because you'll need that release of energy. That's the right time to take an action step, because all of your energy and focus will be in that, which is *so* much more powerful than forcing yourself mentally to do tons of little things before you're ready. Stick around for the singular big things – you'll have all the fuel needed for them, and they will go so much further.

Try this: allow yourself not to work out for a few days – you'll all of a sudden wake up one day and feel a NEED to move. This is the gift in action. Allow your body to tell you when it's the right time to move in everything and embrace your natural stillness in the meantime because it'll tell you everything you need to know.

Simplify your life

The more you strip away temporary phases, obsessions, keeping up with what's cool, the more clearly you'll be able to see. Also pay attention to simplifying your inner world, your thoughts. When you dissolve this mental chatter in yourself, you will make it happen for others – just by being in your energy, they'll feel calmer and more at peace in themselves. This will bleed into everything else you do, whether people are watching you on a screen, hanging out in a space you've created, or coming to your home for a meal. And this is what people will value you for the most.

What Blocks This Gift

Forcing an action plan, believing this is the only way to get things done

Others will tell you that you have to 'focus' and plan your next moves – it's only energetically correct for you to do that if you also have Gift 9. If not, it's actually you living your Design when you're not the one doing that. Maybe someone else in your life brings you that, if you need it. Or you don't get it at all because maybe your life path doesn't need it. Remember that your body will naturally take action when you feel a build-up inside you. And that will be the exact perfect action to take. Achievement is not about how many action steps you take, it's about taking the perfect, Aligned steps, at the perfect, Aligned time for them. If you try to preempt the action, you throw the timing off.

Gift 53
The Starter-Upper

Your favorite thing, and what you're here to do, is start things. You're not necessarily here to finish them (depending on the rest of your gifts). This starter energy can be seen in the big and small things: Maybe you only eat half your plate, maybe you don't ever read the full book – these are all a reflection of this gift, which is being amazing at getting things off the ground and not being so focused on the second half of the process.

It's easier for *every* human being to be most excited at the beginning of something, and anyone can create something, so that in itself is not the gift. Giving it the *best possible start* is the gift. This is what you're here to do – lay great foundations. When you create something, the initial intention and energy you put into it is what dictates how it will go. You've got this gift not to just start for the sake of starting, but to get really strong in your intention for the project and seed that into every part of the foundation.

When you set amazing foundations, your work here is done – you don't have to keep something going, because you've already created such great momentum that will carry that endeavor through so well, and there will be other people with other talents who will bring other things to the table.

How to Flex This Gift

Get clear on what's worth keeping

There are certain things in your life that are worth nurturing and keeping. For example, the relationships you cherish. If you do get bored or uninspired by them, and you're tempted to just move on to new friends, new family, or a new job, think back to your gift: it's about laying good foundations and bringing that energy of newness. From the Universe's point of view, you can do that over and over with the same husband or wife, too, in deeper and deeper levels. Every new height you reach together will require new vibes and new foundations. Try that before moving on to something or someone else. It's not about the outside things changing, it's about *you* constantly bringing that gift to the table.

Don't quit things just because they're getting challenging

There's a difference between knowing when you've made your contribution fully and leaving something because it's become challenging or tough. Maybe things have lost their excitement, and you've become bored: this is not the time to leave necessarily, because you have to learn how to bring excitement from within and put it into whatever you're doing. If you leave to do something else to give you a quick fix of novelty and excitement, you will hit the same walls anyway – this is Life nudging you to look inside.

What Blocks This Gift

Shaming yourself over the fact that you don't finish everything you start

It doesn't matter about what gets completed in the external world so much as what gets accomplished in your internal world. And just like you're a great starter, there are other people in this world who are perfect at finishing things. This is why we all complete each other, and it's beautiful.

But regardless, not everything needs to be finished anyway. And who decides at what point something is 'done' too?

If you've had growth in who you are and have perfected the sharing of your specific gifts, those will always carry over and translate into success in the outside world. And even then, you are the biggest project you will ever accomplish anyway.

Gift 54
Love of Achievement

The process of achieving things and getting rewarded for it excites you. You are a natural grinder and love the process of putting one foot in front of the other to get to where you wanna go. It's not just about the result for you; it's the climb. Climbing puts Life Force inside of you, and when you are excited by something, you can go and go.

You also love seeing the fruits of your labor, whether that's making money, producing great results, or being appreciated or celebrated for what you did, because that dance between what you put in and what you get out – that makes you feel alive.

For you, achievement is not about anyone else. It's a very personal thing – the climb is how you feel good about yourself. It brings you joy and self-esteem. Having something to work toward is good for your Spirit because you are always in your best state when you do. When you pursue something because you love that feeling of putting your energy toward something and then seeing the fruits of your labor come to life, that love is palpable and makes you very attractive – to people, to prospects, to the Universe, which will just send you more and more synchronicities and opportunities and flow so that you can keep grooving in this upward cycle.

How to Flex This Gift

Own your ambition and love of the grind

Society can tell us that ambition is greedy or dog-eat-dog. But those are just the Old Way of being in the world – we wanted to grab everything and suppress everyone to get to the top. Love of achievement is really about being in deep love with your craft and agreeing to make a daily devotion to it. To dance with it regularly and see where it takes you. When you Reframe it as a beautiful thing to scale personal heights, it changes the whole energy around it – including how others receive it, how good it feels to you along the way, and the qualities of doors it opens for you.

What Blocks This Gift

The belief that 'if I can't be the best, there's no point in even trying'

Looking for a guarantee that you'll succeed at something before you even start will paralyze you. Similarly, don't choose something because your mind is convincing you that's the one that's most likely to bring you success. Trust that whatever you're actually excited about the most is the thing the Universe wants you to do. You are built to rise to the top, so be open to whatever the end result looks like – often it can look so much better than your imagination can come up with anyway. Also, for you it's so much more than the result (although you have the drive to make anything succeed when it's Aligned), it's also the inner satisfaction you get from the process. When you have the passion and you embrace the climb, you *will* succeed. If you have something you're truly excited about, try just committing your energy to it and being open to the results being even better than you can imagine.

Keep your eyes on your own plate

Remember that this gift is about your personal relationship with the Universe, with you putting things in and seeing what comes back. So, if you make it about anyone else and look too much at what others are achieving, you will spin out and miss the magic of this gift. Even if you continue to grind and climb, if you're comparing yourself to outside expectations and standards while doing it, the Universe won't bring you as much success as you could otherwise have.

Gift 55
Exuberance

You are someone who feels emotions so fully and strongly, and you have the gift of feeling them more easily than others. Because of this, you have the ability to know how truly incredible and rich the human experience can be – and when you own that knowing, loud and proud, it's contagious.

While the world is so focused on getting things we believe will make us happy, your gift is in reminding us that you could be living your dream life but still not be happy if we haven't opened our hearts and bodies up to the elevated emotional states. An abundant life experience is an inside job.

Feeling exuberant and full of joy is how we all always want to feel, and it's a muscle you can strengthen – you are here to lead the way.

How to Flex This Gift

Learn to accept all your emotional states

You feel the whole spectrum of emotions deeply – that includes the ones that don't feel good, like melancholy and sorrow and sadness. Only once you're willing to look at them can you start to transform them. Name them when you feel them and then realize that they're not permanent, and nor do they say anything about 'you' as a person. Once you see your emotions don't have a grip on you, you can take the 'down' ones less seriously, which then means they don't stick around as long because you're not clinging on to them and creating a story around them. They then simply become visitors that ensure you stay a deep feeler in this world, a sage of emotions that keeps us all in our hearts. And once you have released the grip the low ones have over you, you can spend more time in the good-feeling ones, and the more time you spend in them, the more they grow. This is the forever path of becoming a beacon of joy in the world.

What Blocks This Gift

Judging yourself for having negative feelings or shutting yourself off from them altogether

The world is still so scared of feeling in a deep way – we think it makes us unstable, unintelligent, less capable, and less powerful. But as you're exploring this gift, I bet you're beginning to see how the exact opposite is true. Why every human being wants *anything* is because we believe it will help bring us happiness or avoid sadness and suffering, and this gift is about the fact that these processes are mostly an inside job and that anyone can do them. And by opening yourself up to this possibility, you become a leader toward this kind of human transformation.

So be unapologetic about the way you feel things; you've been given this ability so you can be the lighthouse for all of us.

Gift 56
Feeding the Spirit

You are a spirited person who is here to enrich your own life and other people's lives by communicating with imagination and creativity. People with this gift often are great storytellers and entertainers because this gift is based in the creative, right brain. When you're talking to people, you're not here to just relay the facts – you're here to spark them or make them feel something. If you need to use fantasy and embellishment, you do because this opens up people's imaginations.

This gift is less concerned with what was than what could be. You're not *meant* to communicate so literally, but more in a way that makes people think or feel in a new way. Sometimes, you like to say things that jolt or rouse people, because you love the interplay between different points of view – that helps *you* explore.

In your thoughts, you like to create fantasies and enjoy spending time in the worlds of fiction. It is critical for everyone else's enjoyment of life that you go there. Think of how many people's lives are enriched because J. K. Rowling spread her imagination far and wide.

How to Flex This Gift

Don't judge it

As silly as you may judge this gift, it's a very serious undertaking. Without people like this, we would never be moved to make something better than it is. We need to dream up better versions, create ideals and fantasies that we can then aim toward. We would stay stuck in the scientific, which is also good, but this is the balancing force.

Learn the proper dose of everything

There are no set 'good' or 'bad' things – to eat, do, experience. You are here to master the understanding that things are good for you if they feed and elevate your Spirit in that moment and bad if they don't. Some days a glass of wine will enhance your enjoyment of life, and other times it won't. The key is not coming up with dogmatic laws for yourself to feel safer but to try assessing something in the moment. The more you do this, the more you will trust yourself, and therefore, the more you will feel safe in yourself. Which you need to if you're gonna be open to exploring and trying anything that life has to offer.

What Blocks This Gift

Going to extremes

Because this gift loves to feel stimulated and alive, they can be very prone to stimulating themselves and focusing their attention on too many things that don't actually matter or feed their Spirit. Maybe you spend way too much time scrolling social media, or watching TV, or running from one appointment to the other. It's very important that you keep coming back to the question 'Does this feed my Spirit right now?' to guide you as to whether what you're doing is right for you or whether you're just chasing stimulation for the sake of stimulation. Everything in its right dosage is always the magic for you. Being the right amount of wild, the right amount of fantasist, the right amount of adventurous – that's the wonder of this gift, and if you listen, it will guide you to *your* right amounts.

Gift 57
Reading the Room

These are people who can walk into any room and instantly read the vibes, people, and dynamics between the people. They have strong, predictive, intuitive hunches that come to them instantly – before they've even had time to mentally process it.

Gift 57 is a type of Intuition. If you have it, it means you see, or 'read' the essence of something more easily than you see the thing itself. You just pick up on a feeling or vibe and that's all you need to tell you everything you need to know.

When you trust these feelings without needing to know *why* and *how* you're hearing them, you can let go of needing to have everything figured out (which is a big fixation of yours until you embrace the gift) – you start to see that, in any moment, you know the *next* move, and that's all you ever *need* to know.

You have so many antennae in you that the present situation is literally bursting with intel. You just need to put your full attention on where you are rather than on the imagined scenarios your mind tells you to rehearse or escape to instead. Being fully present, even when it's uncomfortable, is the gift that reaps a thousand more gifts.

You are here to show us that when we soften and relax, all the wisdom and answers come to us – we don't have to push and struggle for them. We've been conditioned to believe that we can only be successful, powerful, and happy by being busy and fast-paced all the time, and you're here to show us the power of softening and quieting.

Once you really relax and just be fully wherever you are, you can feel the truth of the current energy so deeply that you can actually feel what's gonna happen next. It's a gift that's very closely tied to the future, and you have a first look into it.

How to Flex This Gift

Resist the urge to explain away your Intuitive feelings

The key is to understand that you feel things *just because* you feel them. Our culture will make you want to explain yourself, because we believe that smart people can explain their wisdom. You have to embrace the fact that what you pick up on can't ever be fully explained because it's coming from forces so much bigger than you.

What Blocks This Gift

Future tripping

When you're still scared to just relax into your present situation, you can feel this deep fear of the future, which is really a fear of the unknown.

When you're putting your attention on your mind's stories rather than on paying full attention to your current surroundings, you're disconnected from your Intuition, which will create a sense of unease, the opposite of having trust in life, and this will manifest as a constant worry of 'what will happen' and 'what will I do.'

Focusing on the physical world too much

We've been taught to focus so much on the physical as a means of trying to have control over our own lives – what everyone else is doing, saying, the agreed-upon 'reality' we all participate in. The more you can remind yourself that the physical is only a fraction of reality, the more tapped in you will become.

Gift 58
Transforming Dullness into Joy

Gift 58 is all about breathing joy into life. You have this burning desire to make life so great and wonderful, and when you cultivate that in yourself, you exude a joy and vitality that can't help but radiate out of you. Joy is one of the most elevated states of the human experience, and sharing this state is what you're here to do, no matter what costume you wear to do it.

Being fixated by joy and aliveness is how the Universe ensures you keep striving for better, in yourself and for others. So no matter how good things get, you will always go through cycles of feeling dissatisfied with what is, and that is the Universe communicating to you it's time to look around and notice what else could be upgraded or transformed.

The amount of joy you create is directly proportional to the amount you're willing to look at what doesn't feel optimal, without judgment, and look for what changes it's guiding you to make.

How to Flex This Gift

Make friends with the process

The trick with this gift is to embrace how much you want to reach higher heights *without* feeling like nothing is ever good enough. Get your head around the fact that things can always be improved, for as long as you live, so you may as well look at it like a fun and exciting game so that you can have joy at all the points in the journey. It's important to have joy for your everyday things, for simple things, and for being alive itself as well. You can create your dream life, but if you haven't learned to really soak in joy from looking at the stars at night along the way, it won't suddenly come to you once you've reached all your goals.

Also, joy and satisfaction are two different things. No one lives in a permanent state of vivacious exuberance, so don't pressure yourself to live up to that ideal that doesn't exist. It's okay to feel mellow or neutral sometimes too. Top-line joy doesn't matter so much as feeling content and alive deep down. But understand that any bluesiness or melancholy doesn't have to stay a part of your life and is always an opportunity to clean something up so that life can get even better. What a blessing that Life has the potential to keep getting sweeter!

What Blocks This Gift

Disconnecting from your dissatisfaction

In some situations, it can go the other way and instead of fixating on all the things you don't like, you can feel scared to admit you're dissatisfied with something. Because you want joy so badly, sometimes it can make you unwilling to really look at what's *not* making you happy. Perhaps you fear it's unchangeable, so you're scared to even try. Perhaps you feel it would be too painful. But the only way to the joy is through the dissatisfaction. I want to remind you here that you are never stuck, and the sitting with how you truly feel is the first step to regaining total power to transform your life. It will never be too much for you to do; it won't ever be as hard as your mind will imagine it to be; and the Universe always gives you the amount of transformation that you can handle. The gateway to everything you desire is sitting with the truth of how fulfilled or unfulfilled you feel about anything in your life. Eventually, you might find you get excited when you spot dissatisfaction within, because it's pointing you toward the next place where you can create new levels of joy.

Gift 59

Fostering Human Connection

One of your main assets in life is how good you are at getting on well with others and helping them get on well with each other. Creating relationships with people and connecting them to each other is one of your favorite things about life, and it's actually key to your life's Purpose.

For you, it's *necessary* that the central focus of your life is the people. Spending a lot of time maintaining and nurturing your connections, from lovers to acquaintances, will also be the source of your biggest payoffs in life, always. So don't judge yourself for being the one who keeps in touch with even the randomest people, or having a hundred conversations open on your phone, or still having a coffee with that person from middle school. You like to put in a lot of time upfront because of the promise of the connection that could happen.

Plus, it's what you find most enjoyable about life: you live for that feeling of people coming together and having positive interactions – whether that's personal or professional. Not everyone loves people-ing as much as you do. Own this as a superpower.

For you, the feeling really is – What is life if not for the people in it?

How to Flex This Gift

Don't see warmth as a weakness; see it as your particular strength

We've been taught that it's smart to protect yourself and have walls up, and we have to come across like we have it all together, and that we don't *need* people. You are here to embody the opposite in yourself and teach us that too. You can love and adore people and connecting with them, have your guard down, *and also* not lose your own center. You can prioritize socializing with others without ever letting fear or preconceptions they might have of you pull you away.

Let the real 'you' shine

Since connecting and getting on well with others is so important to you, sometimes you can be conditioned that you have to strategize and engineer your interactions to get them to go how you want. But this creates the opposite effect, because it makes you come across as carefully controlled and managed, which prevents them from really feeling the real you.

Relax into bonding rather than pre-think your interactions. Being you, the warmhearted, good-natured you, is the best way to get on with people.

It is so rare in today's world that people lead with that warm and welcoming attitude that we will glue to anyone we see who has it. We will want to be around them, get involved with what they're doing, support what they're selling, etc.

If you've spent your life fronting and getting average levels of connection from it, you might be unwilling to take the risk of *not* fronting and potentially getting worse results. But if you don't try it, you'll never know, and you will always be stuck with the insecurity that you can't be who you are. You can only rid that fear by going and doing the exact opposite. Sure, you might not get on super well with everyone, and in the beginning, you will probably not bond so well with people if you're unsure about your likability because they will be picking up on that, and that affects your bond too. Accept that it'll be a trial and error process, but it's definitely one worth taking because it will enrich your connections and help you love and appreciate all that you really are.

What Blocks This Gift

Distorting your personality

You instinctively know what to say and do in order to make people take a liking to you; and although this is a *kind* of bonding, it's one where you'll never feel truly secure and comfortable because you're taking on an inauthentic persona in order to create the bond. This is a very exhausting way to connect with people because you're having to distort the behavior that would come natural to you all the time – which sucks a lot of your mental energy.

You do this because there's a part of you that doesn't really believe that people could warm to you for who you truly are. And the irony is – you are someone who is naturally so warm and giving that most people won't be able to help loving you, in an even more authentic and magnetic way, when you release the fronting and playing it 'cool' and embrace your *warmth*. Your warmth is your USP, and people always gravitate to us most when we're being the way we're meant to be. All of us are so guarded that we are dying for someone like you to break through all the BS – because that gives *us* permission to relax and be who *we* are. You have a responsibility to become so okay with yourself that you set the tone for all interactions you find yourself in.

Gift 60

Tearing Down Limits

People with this gift are big dreamers but also super realistic and street smart – a potent combination.

You're determined to make stuff happen and are totally intolerant to anything standing in your way – be it rules, restrictions, or red tape. You're here to bust through them, and you have the drive and resilience to back you up.

This gift is about understanding the practicalities of life so clearly. You know how to use boundaries to your advantage: sometimes rules give us a supportive framework within which to create, and sometimes they hold us back. You are great at assessing which is which. What structures are helpful here, and which are holding us back?

This ability makes you the *best* kind of achiever because you're not naive – you assess your situation before you start and then work with what you've got. You see what's standing in the way of achieving any goal and then see the way to tear it down.

You are the ultimate 'when life gives you lemons, make lemonade.' But if you've got grapes, you're gonna make a kick-ass grape juice.

Resilience and resourcefulness are the names of your game.

How to Flex This Gift

Embrace your impatience

You have an intolerance for roadblocks, and you get a high from busting through them – this is the Universe's way of telling you to keep doing more of this.

Sometimes this intolerance for roadblocks can make you impatient, but it's a *good* kind of impatience driving you to dissolve the blocks and come out on the other side.

However, there's a difference between impatience at the rules, the framework, the structure, and impatience at people. Sometimes you'll find yourself getting frustrated that other people are being 'too slow' or 'not getting it'; but remember that they don't have the same gifts as you and are working at their own Divine pace. You are meant to be the one who clears stuff out of the way for all of us, which you wouldn't be able to do if everyone knew how to do it.

What Blocks This Gift

Don't ever get discouraged when you feel a limitation, use it as fuel to bust through it

It's easy to let the restrictions and limitations make you feel helpless or powerless. Don't; it's all here to help you. When something appears to stand in your way, realize it says nothing about you or your potential. It's not happening to you to hold you back, it's happening to stoke your fire, to reinvigorate your drive. Changing your perspective from blocks being negative to being positive is often the biggest and only shift required for you to really be in this gift. These roadblocks are a blessing because they keep you on the path of being who you are, which is a person who's always wanting to expand and evolve.

Gift 61

Inner Knowing

You are a curious person who's always looking for answers, for truth. This need-to-know drives you to uncover deeper and deeper layers of understanding about things that interest you.

Sometimes, you'll use these understandings to further other people's understandings too. But also, your new levels of understanding will always bleed into everything you do, because you'll be doing them with a different level of consciousness. So, it's affecting other people either way, whether directly or indirectly.

When you get an inner knowing about something, it's clear and hard to miss, like a download or lightning bolt you feel that hits you through your core. When you see or feel something True, you know it in your bones.

Gift 61 is about this special inner radar for Truth; you sniff it from a mile away. And it's not about having all the facts; it happens when you quiet all the outside noise and tune in to what you feel is the Truth. As you grow, you'll see that Truth reveals itself to you on the inside not the outside world of facts and information. So the irony with this inner knowing is that, when you stop this constant searching, everything you want and need to know comes flooding into you.

And the thing about Truth with a capital *T* is it's not fixed. As we evolve, so *it* evolves. Stay open to new levels of truths and knowings that can keep revealing themselves to you deeper and deeper if you let them.

How to Flex This Gift

Don't try to justify it to others

Just because you can't prove or justify something, it doesn't make it any less valid. Resist the urge to prove Truths based on the outside world's standards and stick strong to what the inner radar says. Sometimes you won't be able to explain it, and that's okay. What matters is that *you* trust you. Your inner knowing is a direct connection to the Divine, which is a precious asset that has higher levels of intelligence that science only wishes it could access.

What Blocks This Gift

Distraction

Looking for answers on the outside is good when the information serves you and your Purpose. It's *not* so good when the outside searching is a compulsion or distraction that prevents you from looking inside for what that radar says. So ask – 'Is this knowledge that feeds me, or is it knowledge I'm needing to feel secure, smart, or worthy?'

Needing a final answer as a resting place

Don't blindly subscribe to a system that claims to have all the answers – whether that's a religion, a spiritual system, or a science. This is wrong because your knowing is meant to constantly renew and evolve as your mind expands. So, hanging your hat on a final answer for *anything* will always hold you back. In today's world, having the final answer can feel like a safety blanket, because knowing makes us feel like we have control. But the real safety is letting Life guide you to a higher perspective at every turn when your consciousness is ready for its next upgrade. And the more you let that happen, the safer you'll feel in the truth that the Universe, the unseen forces, are always at play for good in your life.

Gift 62
Eclectic Knowledge

You are the person among your friendship group who knows and remembers random facts about so many niche and diverse things. At the heart of this gift, there are things in this world that make all the sense in the world to you, where to everyone else, they just don't. Usually, when something is random, unusual, or doesn't fit into the way most of us like to see the world, we reject it. These are the very things that you absolutely adore and 'get.'

This gift is focused on your natural grasp of things rather than 'taught' knowledge. But make no mistake – you are highly intelligent, just in a way that is more progressive than our current status quo.

If this seems useless to you, know that it's not. When you allow yourself to absorb things that interest you, you'll see that they always come in handy later down the line in some fashion. You just can't see how yet, but don't let that ever make you feel like this is not an unbelievable gift.

How to Flex This Gift

Own your heart's knowledge

Tell from the heart rather than actual facts. Reminder: you are not here to be a human textbook. You are here to share what you do know, what makes sense to you in your heart, and not worry about what you don't know. Don't doubt the truths you have faith in, deep in your bones – even when the world hasn't caught up to them yet.

Make facts exciting by bringing them to life

Your gift is in making the facts you *do* know exciting; words are magic, and you have a unique way of expressing things. Use it to your advantage! You always shine and are most impactful when you tell people in an animated, impassioned way rather than just reciting the dry explanation.

Think of words as tools that help you do your real work, which is to get across a feeling or a heart-based grasp rather than just telling the facts themselves. That's what you're here to do, and what people will appreciate you for the most. Let your enthusiasm shine through unabashedly – when you see it as a strength, you make it more likely for others to interpret it as a strength too. Whereas, when we're still doubting it, it creates more room for others to judge, doubt, and dismiss it. Give it the full spotlight.

Don't ever question your interests in things – they're not 'random'; they are Divine

The Universe *made* you interested in those things for a purpose. The things that are right for you to share are the ones that you find relevant, not the things you're sharing because everyone else is and expects you to do the same. Maybe that expectation to conform comes from you putting that pressure on yourself, too, based off of what you see other people in your industry or on social media talking about. You will always be your most magnetic when you go against the grain and write that fictional story about aliens, create the Japanese manga stickers, or talk about whatever floats your boat in that interview rather than saying the stock phrases everyone else says, no matter how enlightened or progressive those stock phrases may sound. Let yourself go left-of-center.

What Blocks This Gift

Focusing on anything to avoid focusing on the things your Soul wants you to

People with this gift sometimes use their ability to absorb (and get lost in) so many details as a distraction tactic to delay being in their greatness. Getting lost in the details of unhelpful things can become an (unconscious) way of procrastinating from being in your greatness.

When you catch yourself getting lost in fixating and analyzing things that don't really matter *to you*, you will free up more energy to communicate from the heart.

Gift 63
Exploring the Unknown

Gift 63s are always asking questions about life. They love to wonder what else they don't yet know and always leave room for new knowledge to come into their lives. And usually, in their quest for answers, these people reach better ways of seeing things and new levels of information. In doing so, they advance our collective thirst for inspiration and information.

This gift isn't about getting the answers; it's about the fact that you extend your mind past the normal edges so that it can ponder the mysterious, uncharted edges of what we collectively know. At your best, you *love* the unknown and are comfortable in it. When you cultivate a deep trust in Life, in forces greater than yourself, the unknown becomes a fun frontier ripe for our discovery and delight. This is the Spirit you're designed to live in and lead others into as well.

What gives you this seeking mind is your healthy dose of questioning things. You don't settle for taking things at face value and always want to see more – which ensures you have an independence of thought, and in today's world of homogenization and sameness, that's a huge value.

How to Flex This Gift

Honor your doubts

Sit with your doubts; listen to them, entertain them. It's actually running from the doubts and ignoring them that will keep you from advancing. Doubts aren't always as 'bad' as society makes them out; pondering and questioning things is given to you on purpose as a way of pushing you to reach for higher levels of information and understanding.

The magic is in entertaining your doubts instead of shutting them down. Because once you've asked new questions, you've made space to receive new answers.

Listen to the right doubts

Like all gifts, this one thrives when you don't use it all up on your personal life. You're meant to look out at life and ponder things that interest you, to get new thoughts, concepts, and wisdom. But as for your personal life, we're not *meant* to ask for answers about how it's going to unfold, because it would rob us of the mystery of life. When you doubt your future, you will feel powerless; when you use this gift on subjects that fascinate you, and you witness your gift in action, you will feel strong and competent.

What Blocks This Gift

Internalizing other people's doubts

Since you're tuned in to the energy of doubt, you can also sense when people are doubting themselves. Just make sure you don't take those on or mistake them as your own.

When you feel unsure of yourself, ask: Is this coming from your own self-doubt or are you feeling other people doubting you or themselves? This can either be from the present, so from people around you, or historical, a.k.a. ingrained in you from doubtful people whose energy you internalized in the past.

Gift 64
The Finish Line

This gift creates the happy, peaceful ending. You are an expert at making sure conversations, creations, or projects are finished properly, and actually prefer the destination to the journey. What's more, you won't close any chapter until you feel like you got something from it – whether that's a lesson, an answer, a tying up of loose ends.

Your brain is always wondering: 'What was it all for? What does it amount to? What's the lesson here?' And because you ask these questions, you bring us clarity around situations to help make sense of everything that happened.

The fact that you don't leave any stone unturned is a *good* thing in you. There has to be a point to it all. At the deepest level, this is very philosophical, because Gift 64 is the last of all the gifts.

On the macro level, it represents the deep human need for us to look back on the end of our lives and know it all served a purpose.

How to Flex This Gift

Learn to live with uncertainty while things are in the thick of evolution

The clarity you seek won't be in endlessly analyzing or trying to explain it away, but in being attentive enough to life that, when the Universe is trying to send you the answers, you can receive it. Don't grasp for clarity, just clear your mind and observe. While waiting for the ending or answers to come, you can practice trusting that it always will, and at the perfect time, if you're open. Think of a time(s) in your life when things seemed unclear and then all of a sudden, it came together and got tied up so beautifully. If you've seen it before, it's easier to *know* that this is just the cycles of life.

Get okay with things seeming in dis-order

Before you get to the end point, things won't seem to fit into nice, neat little boxes – it only does when you get there and look back. Don't give up when things seem uncertain; keep engaging with life and doing your part, and when the time is right, you will have tied everything up in the most beautiful (and concise) bow, without really knowing how it all orchestrated so perfectly.

What Blocks This Gift

Fear of leaving a current cycle

Endings can be scary because then you wonder what's next. It can therefore feel safer to be looking for the answer than in having the answers. The finish line of one project, one question, one journey isn't the ending of it all, it's simply the foundation on which the next journey will begin. The end becomes the new beginning; and so continues the cycles of rebirth and renewal. We are always in the process, even when we come to the 'ends'; Life will always have more and higher for us to go.

Remember that lack of clarity says nothing about you

In those moments when you don't have clarity (yet), make sure not to think it's because you lack knowledge, understanding, or capability – you don't always have the answer. Don't let the conditioned fear of actually just experiencing life, with all its mess and chaos, make you hide from life. Just jump in and have faith that it is all going to amount to something.

Once you accept that, you'll be able to review and conclude, sum up a project, an era, or experiment better than anyone. In order to *master* the cycles, you have to be *in* the cycles.

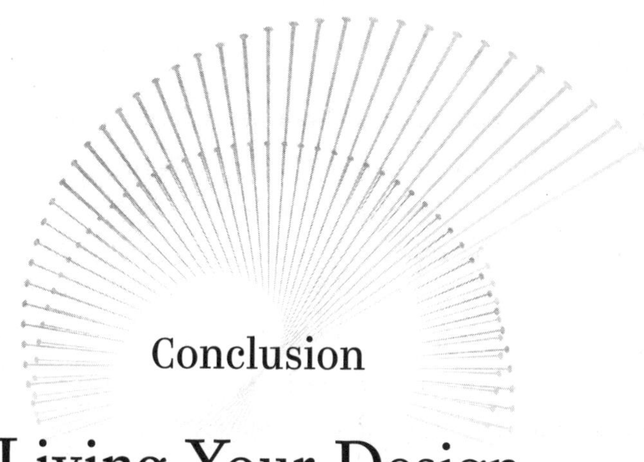

Conclusion
Living Your Design

We're constantly bombarded with ideas of what to be; I hope this book brings you back to remembering *your* way to be. I hope it frees you of wasting your mental and physical energy, trying to do it any other way than your preexisting, Divinely designed way. Remembering who you are is 90 percent of the work so you can live from your Essence.

When you're trying to make changes to live your Design, it can be overwhelming, and you might wonder where to even start; I recommend picking the things you're most drawn to. When you see how those things create positive shifts in your life, it gives you evidence that this tool really works, and that will build a natural momentum that will carry you forward.

There is no right or wrong way to do this. Each person will read this book and work with it in a different way, and that's how it *should* be, because, as we've learned, there is no one-size-fits-all. There is no 'right' order to do it in either, only the right order for you: your natural inclinations will guide you to your perfect process if you just do what you feel pulled to do in this moment and then the next.

Becoming the real you is not an overnight sensation; you have your whole life to take it higher and higher, and there will always be new levels you can reach. Always just take the next step and then keep taking the one after that. That's how you build a strong foundation.

Live *your* way of being and radiate that out into the world. What makes people magnetic is not any one quality in itself – you only have to look at different people you find magnetic to notice the range of characteristics they display. What makes people magnetic is when they have a strong sense of who they are and live from that center.

When you are strong in your picture of your True Self, you aren't swayed by the constant (overt and implied) ways you're being told to be otherwise.

Human Design is often called an experiment. It's an invitation to not just take my word for all you've read about yourself, but to really try and see the results or changes it brings to your life.

This work really shines when you share it with others too.

Accepting others is understanding that what's correct for them is totally different than what's correct for you.

Unless you truly *see* the other for who they are, any acceptance of them can only go so deep. Whereas, when you peek under the hood and see their machinations, you will see their innocent motives, you will see there's a very good reason why they do the things they do, and you will see how the things that feel abrasive are because they're acting out their conditioning sometimes rather than their True Self.

Learning who the other person is and realizing exactly how they're different than you brings so much acceptance. And acceptance is the building block of loving others. Not loving them because you try to with your mind but because you see them.

I hope this book helps you understand that your natural traits are your best you.

I hope it helps you have compassion for all the times you've tried to be anything else.

I hope it frees you from ever entertaining the idea that you should contort yourself to be a certain way.

I hope it frees you to be exactly who you came here to be.

And not just because it's a life that brings more ease, success, and joy. But because being the highest expression of yourself is precisely what will serve others the most.

Acknowledgments

The most important thank you is to You, the person reading this. You can't have picked up this book without having already embarked on a journey of consciousness and growth. It's because of people like you that we WILL have a world in which people are their Real Selves, live in deep love and connection with others, create scientifically measurable magic in our own specific ways, and elevate together. Living for us on this shared mission, all playing our unique part, is my Why.

To the Hay House family – thank you for breathing life and reality into what was just a word stream in my head, and trusting me to deliver something that belonged amongst the incredible legacy that you make in this world.

To Ra – thank you for showing me the way. I hope I'm making you proud.

Manex – you are my spirit guide but in this world. Thank you for showing me the magic, hidden right here in the human-ness.

Tita – you opened the doors of my inner world way before I even knew I had one.

Ruth – thank you for being my first and most present mentor and teacher.

Dara – thank you for pushing me into this edge and many others for my greatest good.

Amelia, Sarah, Karina, Krista, Jordan, and Jonathan – thank you for being my co-conspirators.

Jane – I couldn't imagine a bigger gift to have been given than you.

Taylor – I thank my lucky stars that you just magically appeared that day.

To my Family: Mama, Papa, Andrew, and Sofia – I'm so grateful for us each being radically unusual but doing it together. It's the greatest strength and the greatest joy.

To my sister – this is for us.

© Jenna Zoë

About the Author

Jenna Zoë is a world-leading expert in Human Design. She presents it through a lens of acceptance and spiritual understanding, which has resonated with millions around the globe and turned it into a mainstream obsession. Her main goal is to help people truly understand who they are and how they function, so they can spend their energy becoming the greatest expression of their unique gifts and talents, rather than trying to be who they were told to be.

She has built a library of online courses about Human Design, formal trainings for people who want to make it a career, and made the My Human Design app so that knowing yourself and everyone in your life becomes a seamless part of your every day.

myhumandesign.com

@jennazoe and **@my.humandesign**

CONNECT WITH

HAY HOUSE

ONLINE

hayhouse.co.uk

@hayhouse

@hayhouseuk

@hayhouseuk

@hayhouseuk

@hayhouseuk

Find out all about our latest books & card decks • Be the first to know about exclusive discounts • Interact with our authors in live broadcasts • Celebrate the cycle of the seasons with us • Watch free videos from your favourite authors • Connect with like-minded souls

'The gateways to wisdom and knowledge are always open.'

Louise Hay